Don & Sandra Humphrey
3705 Priest Lake Drive
Nashville, TN 37217

Free to Grieve

Free to Grieve

MAUREEN RANK

BETHANY HOUSE PUBLISHERS
MINNEAPOLIS, MINNESOTA 55438
A Division of Bethany Fellowship, Inc.

Published by Bethany House Publishers
A Division of Bethany Fellowship, Inc.
6820 Auto Club Road, Minneapolis, MN 55438

Printed in the United States of America

Library of Congress Cataloging in Publication Data

Rank, Maureen.
  Free to grieve.

  Bibliography: p.
  1. Miscarriage—Psychological aspects. 2. Stillbirth—Psychological aspects. 3. Grief. 4. Bereavement—Psychological aspects. I. Title.
RG648.R36   1985   155.9'37   85-11273
ISBN 0-87123-806-3

DEDICATION

mentor (men´tĕr), n: a close, trusted, and experienced counselor or guide.

To my husband, Mike, and my brother, Russ—mentors to me in the richest sense.

THE AUTHOR

MAUREEN RANK is a writer and seminar speaker with a degree in Home Economics and Family Relations from Iowa State University. She and her husband worked with the Navigators and now make a home for their two children in Knoxville, Iowa.

ACKNOWLEDGMENTS

Thanks to Phyllis Adams, Kristy Defenbaugh, Myrl Glockner, Mary Koehlor, Joy Lane, Lynette Melcher, Jan Stowe, and the many other women who so freely shared their lives and stories with me. In nearly every case, the women's names were changed and certain details fictionalized in order to protect their privacy.

And I am grateful to the health care professionals who generously contributed their expertise: Barbara Batts, M.D.; Diane Bierke-Nelson, M.S., M.S.S.W.; Robert Bremner, M.D.; Charles R. King, M.D.; and Kurt R. Vander Ploeg, M.D.

A special thanks is also due to my sister, Margie Kuiper, and to Nathan Unseth of Bethany Fellowship, for encouragement through the gestation and delivery of this book.

TABLE OF CONTENTS

INTRODUCTION

"You Shouldn't Cry . . ."

Jill Taylor drove home from her obstetrician's office wrapped in the same warm glow of success she had felt the day she got her master's degree. The pregnancy test—positive! She was going to have another baby.

So many good things had come together for them this year; they almost didn't deserve another. The challenge of her husband Ben's new job in commodities more than made up for his hour-long commute to downtown Chicago each day. And after four years of apartment dwelling, the Taylors had finally become homeowners. Jill had begun pounding nails with abandon into the walls of their newly purchased house in a sleepy Chicago suburb. Her career as a special ed teacher shelved for now, Jill was relishing the time to expand her interests that full-time mothering afforded. Learning quilting, studying the home schooling movement, keeping up with their firstborn Matthew's inexhaustible exhuberance. And now anticipating being the mother of two.

Jill's pregnancy had come right on schedule. Matthew had just turned twenty-one months, so he would be two-and-a-half when the new baby came. Just the spacing all her parenting books recommended. Her Cuban-born parents had raised seven children, so Jill had always envisioned herself surrounded by a laughing, bouncing brood of her own. Maybe she and Ben wouldn't make it to seven, but at least they were now one closer

11

to their own semblance of a clan.

By the second prenatal appointment, Ben, too, had relaxed about the prospect of another baby. As an only child, he hadn't seriously considered the fact that he might father more than one offspring. But both he and Jill were thinking Baby by now. Jill wasn't as sick as she'd been with Matthew, he noted. Maybe she was getting the hang of this pregnancy thing.

The second checkup came and went. The doctor couldn't hear the baby's heartbeat, but Jill shrugged it off. After all, she recalled, there hadn't been an audible heartbeat with Matthew until four months. And the doctor didn't appear concerned, though he did ask that she return in two weeks to check again for the heartbeat, "just to be on the safe side."

The morning of that appointment, Jill began to feel pains, almost like light menstrual cramps. "Maybe it's good I see the doctor today," she thought. By the time she left the house, she was cramping enough that it was work to climb the steps to her sitter's front door. She was uncomfortable, but not afraid. Probably a stomach flu or something. Seeing the doctor would take care of it.

The nurse seemed to hedge the subject of Jill's cramps as she took the vitals and then checked for the baby's heartbeat. Failing to hear it, she called in another nurse to have a try. Jill watched uninvolved, half-distracted by the intermittent cramping and impatient to have the exam over. "Maybe the doctor will have better luck," the nurse frowned and went to call him.

Jill chafed a bit at the doctor's time-consuming thoroughness as he moved his stethoscope slowly over her abdomen. They hadn't heard Matthew's heartbeat this early, and the issue at hand was getting relief from these cramps, not following all the steps of a proper prenatal exam. The doctor put down his stethoscope and turned to his nurse, "We're going to do a pelvic," he announced flatly and slipped on surgical gloves.

A pelvic? Jill winced. Those exams were the least favorite part of the prenatal experience for her. She didn't expect another pelvic until close to the end of the pregnancy. Why was he ordering one now? The poking and pushing seemed even less tolerable than usual, and she tightened her hold on the examination table.

The doctor finished, stripped off his gloves and handed them to his nurse. "Mrs. Taylor," he said as he turned to her, "you're going to miscarry, probably within the week. So . . . go home and do it." And he walked out.

Jill stared after him. She would lose the baby? She was going to miscarry? What did that . . . but the doctor had gone on to another patient. Somehow she dressed and stumbled out of the office bewildered and frightened.

When she got home, Jill instinctively reached for the phone to call Ben. "Ben . . . the baby. The doctor says we're going to lose it. And I'm having these cramps and I'm so scared."

Ben didn't know enough about miscarriages to determine what questions to ask, but he did know when Jill was in trouble. He stopped just long enough to call his mother in Iowa, asking her to come, and boarded the next commuter train for home. When he rushed through the front door an hour and an eternity later, Jill was panic-stricken. She had begun to bleed and the cramping was worse. The blood flow wasn't profuse—much like a heavy period—but for someone with no idea of what was ahead, it conjured up images of hemorrhaging.

By the time the Taylors pulled up to the emergency room, Jill was hyperventilating, less from the pain than from unbridled fear. The cramps were coming in waves, hard and heavy. Since Jill's first delivery had been Caesarean, she had never experienced the building intensity of labor pains, so she had no idea how long the pulling, tearing sensation inside would continue to worsen.

Once in a hospital room, Jill rested in bed between trips to the bathroom to pass blood and clots into the stool. She felt calmer now, more in control, partly because a mild sedative was taking effect and partly because of the reassurance of help close at hand. The cramping seemed less intense than it had in the emergency room. Maybe the baby was pulled loose, she mulled, and now I'm just waiting for it to come out. Anyway, the worst seemed to be over. Ben was with her until about nine o'clock that night, when he left to meet his mother at the bus depot. Jill felt comfortable with him going; things seemed to be moving more slowly now.

About ten minutes after Ben had gone, Jill felt the urge again to go to the bathroom. But this time, the clot came out with a big "plop" into the stool. It was smaller than her fist, but obviously a mass of tissue. For Jill there was a sense of relief, like a difficult job finished. She called a nurse, who confirmed that the miscarriage had actually taken place.

"I want to see the baby," Jill told her. The nurse was surprised. "Are you sure, honey? It probably wouldn't be the best. It might make for more difficulty later." But Jill insisted. Now that the terror of the miscarriage was over, she felt like nothing new could be as bad. And by now her natural instincts of insatiable curiosity had returned. She had never seen a developing fetus, and she wanted to see what one looked like. This was a woman, after all, who spent some of her first months of married life juggling orders as a Denny's waitress, not out of economic necessity, but because she simply had to know what it felt like to be a waitress.

The nurse brought the baby in. It was only the size of a quarter, Jill observed, but so much was perfectly formed—little arms and legs, tiny eyes. A few days later, when the meaning of her loss had begun to register, Jill could never have been so cool about seeing the tiny body. But at the time her response seemed perfectly natural.

The next day, her doctor performed a D and C,[1] and the following morning she went home. Miscarriage over.

But for Jill, the miscarriage was far from over. The baby had physically separated from her, but the emotional tearing away had barely begun. All the courage and peace she had felt as she looked at the tiny fetus in the hospital somehow ebbed away, and in its place a terrible sadness took residence. Jill would wait until her son and mother-in-law left for their afternoon walk each day and then shed tears that would not stop. One day a blossoming pregnant lady; a few days later flat and empty, the baby gone.

A heavy aching filled Jill's heart and would not lift. "Could I have caused the miscarriage?" she asked herself, remembering the room she'd painted early in the pregnancy. Hadn't she won-

---

[1]Dilation and curettage—a procedure in which the cervix is dilated, and the uterus scraped. Because of most women's familiarity with the term, it will be referred to by the commonly used abbreviation, D and C, throughout this book.

dered about exposure to the paint fumes? And hadn't her sisters told her not to lift Matthew while she was pregnant, because they thought the weight of a two-year-old could cause the pregnancy to tear loose? Did this mean there might not be more children? She was, after all, thirty-three. Maybe Matthew's birth had just been a lucky fluke, and more tries at pregnancy would also end in failure. Guilt and fear weighed heavily upon her but not nearly as heavily as a sickening sadness.

"It wasn't depression I was experiencing," Jill recalled, "but a period of mourning. This was my first experience of losing someone I loved. And I really grieved."

But others around her saw no need to grieve. There was the not-so-subtle-finger-pointing from her family ("I told you what would happen if you lifted too much, but you wouldn't listen."). But just as difficult to deal with were the well-intentioned don't-be-sad niceties others offered. "You have a strong faith," one solicited. "You'll get over it." "You shouldn't cry. You'll have other children," another assured. "Will I?" Jill wanted to scream. "How do *you* know?"

One neighbor came calling and spent the entire visit gossiping about goings-on in the neighborhood. "I know she meant well," Jill said later, "because it was a technique I had used myself when I couldn't face another person's sadness. She was trying to distract me from the loss. But what I wanted more than anything was to talk about the baby's death." The woman finally left, and Jill did her crying alone.

Three weeks after the miscarriage, Jill began to feel like herself again physically, and Ben's mother went home. To the outside world, she was functioning normally once again. But it was almost six months before the private work of grief was done.

Not that she cried for six months. Life did go on. But there were moments, unexpected moments, when Jill's sadness resurfaced and almost consumed her. Like the Sunday when the minister mentioned people having children and Jill began to cry, quietly at first and then with less control. She desperately wanted to leave, but was sandwiched in the middle of a long row of people. So she choked back sobs and endured the service to its end.

Another time that fall she was caught off guard by her anger at a friend's pregnancy announcement. Release from the weight of hurt and anger she felt inside was slow in coming.

I too have known the searing disappointment of a lost pregnancy. In the process of getting our two children, we lost five others. And each year, nearly one million women will experience the pain of a lost pregnancy. Despite the frequency of this problem, most will find it is a subject little talked about. And often it is an experience for which only minimal grieving is considered acceptable. Nonetheless, thousands of women know that the pain of miscarriage or stillbirth does not "just go away." Months after, they still struggle with a peculiar kind of hurt other people find hard to understand or accept. It is for these women, looking for answers to their questions and healing for their wounds, that this book has been written.

SECTION ONE:
LEARNING TO GRIEVE

CHAPTER ONE

A Peculiar Kind of Hurt

Women who lose pregnancies sometimes feel frightened, other times guilty, often confused, but nearly always very alone.

What is the pain of this loss? And why so much pain?

It is unexpected.

In an age of medical miracles, we've come to expect that pregnancies end in, of course, babies. But as a specialist in high-risk pregnancies observed, "A hundred years ago, a pregnant woman knew it was questionable that she'd finish the pregnancy with a healthy child in her arms. A miscarriage or stillbirth was, perhaps, less painful because expectations weren't as high."

My mother bore six children, and all four of my sisters-in-law routinely conceived and delivered right on schedule. At the time of my first miscarriage, I could not name one person I knew who had lost a child before birth. I equated "pregnant" with the guarantee of a baby. (After my third unsuccessful pregnancy, I recall deciding to announce "I am pregnant," rather than "We're going to have a baby." By that time I knew how much blind faith those we're-having-a-baby assertions really involve.)

Yet despite our present-day world of medical miracles, pregnancy loss could be called the "unheralded epidemic." One third of all women who conceive children have at least one miscarriage.[1] And the National Center for Health Statistics reports that

---

[1]Alan Nourse, M.D., *Ladies' Home Journal Family Medical Guide* (New York: Harper and Row, 1973), p. 818.

these losses touch nearly one million couples every year.[2] Other sources put the number somewhat lower, closer to 600,000, but in either case, most women who have been through a miscarriage or stillbirth are astonished when they realize how many other women like them there must be.[3]

In light of the frequency of miscarriage, it is surprising that physicians rarely mention to their prenatal patients the possibility of losing a pregnancy. As one obstetrician explained, "The odds are greatest that a woman won't miscarry. Why worry her with a possibility which more times than not *doesn't* occur?"

He has a point, of course. But one of the factors adding to the trauma of miscarriage is that most often the couple is completely unprepared for it. When a loved one dies after a long illness, there has been the chance to slowly adjust to the idea of death. But when the death is sudden and unexpected, as in miscarriage, there is no time for gradually accepting the reality of that loss.

It's not talked about.

"Just where *are* all these women who've lost babies?" one anguished mother demanded. "I don't think anyone I know has been through miscarriage besides me."

Her complaint points out one of the key factors that gives pregnancy losses their peculiar kind of hurt. It is a life experience women often don't talk about. Why not? There are several reasons.

A woman may feel ashamed. She has failed somehow, she tells herself—failed herself, her husband, and most of all, her child. Clemson University sociologists who studied mothers in mourning observed that feelings of anger and bitterness were more commonly expressed by mothers whose children died after birth. But women who miscarried or delivered stillborn babies felt guilt and failure more intensely. And most people are not quick to publicize what they perceive as their failures.

---

[2]Susan O. Borg and Judith Laske, *When Pregnancy Fails* (Boston: Beacon Press, 1981), pp. 8, 9.

[3]Joseph Carey, "Loving—and Mourning—Your Baby," *USA Today* (April 10, 1984).

Also, women who are reticent to talk about their experiences may be taking a cue from the generation before them which never talked openly about such matters as pregnancy. I just discovered a year ago that an older friend wasn't childless by choice—she had been through multiple miscarriages. While we had talked about many things, she never mentioned that fact, even though she knew I was struggling with the same problem. She was simply too embarrassed to mention miscarriage; it would be almost as personal as telling me about her sex life.

For reasons such as these, some women don't readily own up to pregnancy loss, so the woman going through the experience feels isolated.

Miscarriage may be your first experience with death.

Like Jill and Ben, many younger parents who lose a pregnancy are experiencing their first encounter with death. You never get used to death, but losing someone you love does push you up against realities that otherwise can be shelved for another day. Having grieved once can give, as it were, grieving skills. The process of mourning will still accompany each miscarriage, but at least there will be greater opportunity to cooperate with that process, once you have experienced it.

After the death of her mother, a woman talked about the working-out of her grief. "Having always been so happy, grieving still seemed utterly strange to me—foreign, unfamiliar. . . . But now something is changing. You see, all this time it didn't seem *real* that my mom was gone—really gone. I'd walk through the stores downtown where we'd shopped together so often, and it didn't seem real that she wasn't trotting along beside me. . . . It didn't seem plausible that anything had changed! Now, after more than two years without her, at last I *know* and recognize my *aloneness.* A better word is 'apartness.' Like Alice and the Red Queen, I've crossed a brook. I'm on into the next square. Reality is all around me, and I sense in myself a new tenderness, a new awareness. (Mocking birds even sound different.) I am essentially alone, and this is real to me. I'm not complaining. That is just it. It's ā certain peace and a sureness I never knew before. Suddenly I've almost stopped *questioning*."[4]

Another death may not wound this woman in the same way, because she has now confronted grief squarely, and acquired inner resources she lacked before. But many women who miscarry have never experienced a loved one's death, so they come to the experience more vulnerable than they might be at another point in life.

You may feel you have failed to fulfill an adult responsibility.

Pregnancy losses, particularly miscarriages, occur most often at the beginning and the ending of reproductive life. More teenagers and women in their late thirties go through losses than women in the middle child-bearing years. And this loss may pack even more of a wallop for these age groups because of what else is happening during these particular life stages.

Any woman in her late teens or early twenties sits in the midst of a formidable list of life tasks. Yale's Daniel Levinson describes the work of these early twenties as "making a place in the Adult World." Such a woman is often leaving the nest to establish one of her own. She is defining what a grown-up is and is struggling to prove that she can really be one. Mothering children may well be a part of that scenario for her.

For Denise, part of showing she was mature involved being able to give children to her husband, who desperately wanted to be a father. Consequently, their daughter's stillbirth screamed "Failure!" with double force. Denise not only had the baby to mourn, but also her own inability to do what she so very much wanted to do. Though there is usually the option of another try, a first bump up against such a disappointment can cut deeply.

Pregnancy loss may mean the end of your baby chances.

For the woman at the other end of the reproductive spectrum, there are struggles, too, but different ones. Unlike her

---

[4]Eugenia Price, *No Pat Answers* (New York: Bantam Books, 1972), pp. 39, 40.

twenty-year-old sister, a woman in her late thirties groans over wrinkles around her eyes that night creams won't smooth away. And she may notice that age is catching up to her parents. Her self-sufficient mom doesn't feel up to having the whole family over for Thanksgiving anymore. And her Dad can't remember where he puts things; though he laughs it off, she can tell it scares him a little. A baby means something different now. For such a woman, it speaks reassuringly of the continuity of life. She fears that with this loss she may also have lost the chance to ever have children—or more children. Unlike the twenty-year-old, she is keenly aware of the fact that reproductive life doesn't go on forever.

Others don't know how to respond.

Miscarriage is a sadness that must too often be borne alone, because the people who love the woman just don't know she needs help.

Some view miscarriage as they do an appendectomy; a body part that didn't function correctly had to be removed. And they expect you to feel relieved. When Tom and Mary met their doctor at the emergency room just after Mary had miscarried, he asked how she was feeling. "I'm mostly sad, I guess," Mary told him. "We're just so disappointed about losing the baby."

"Wait, now," the doctor interrupted. "You can't think of this as losing a baby—it was a fetus, a mass of cells. What you lost was just tissue, not a person." Mary was left with her sadness, as well as guilt because she felt sad. She and Tom later learned through a newspaper report that the doctor's clinic performed more abortions than any other in the city. His "it wasn't a baby" rationale may have satisfied elective aborters, but for Mary it only blocked the natural grief she felt at the death of her child.

While some doctors may not offer much emotional support, sometimes family and friends do little better.

Sociologists Larry Peppers and Ronald Knapp explain, "The mother finds herself in an extremely undesirable situation. She suffers intense grief, and she does so in virtual isolation. Even her husband cannot always comprehend the depth of her feelings, particularly in the case of a miscarriage. Her parents and other relatives, her friends and acquaintances, and in some cases even her physician, all respond with limited and short-lived compassion.

"In fact, the usual sympathies that are extended to individuals who lose a spouse, a parent, or an older child are generally not offered to parents who have lost an infant, particularly if the loss occurred in the prenatal period before the child was viable and observable. The feelings on the part of others seem to be that since the child was unknown, its death cannot be tragic. Therefore they encourage the grieving mother to 'Get well! You can have others.' "[5]

Lou's mother had miscarried several times, so when she came to visit right after Lou's miscarriage, her daughter anticipated being able to open up about her feelings with someone who understood. But her mom had never talked about her own miscarriages. She'd gotten through with a stiff-upper-lip approach, as if admitting that they hurt would only make the hurt worse. So she refused to listen whenever Lou tried to talk about what had happened, instead changing the subject. Finally the tension of this dodging act became too much. Lou's mother insisted to her husband that they cut their visit short. Maybe she was trying to shield herself from sadness or doing what she thought best for Lou—diverting her from the unpleasant. "Whatever her reason, I felt so rejected," Lou said.

Sometimes grieving friends don't know what to say, so they say nothing. When my mother died, a girl I'd been close to for several years took no initiative at all toward me. I was surprised and disappointed, wondering why she didn't care when we'd shared so much in the past. Later she told me, "It wasn't that I didn't feel for you—perhaps I felt too much. My dad died several years ago, and his death did, and still does, overwhelm me. I couldn't bear to think of you going through sorrow like that, especially when I saw no way to help. So I stayed away." That friend's response to my grief perhaps mirrors the reactions of

---

[5]Larry G. Peppers and Ronald J. Knapp, *Motherhood and Mourning, Perinatal Death* (New York: Praeger Publishers, 1980), pp. 28–29.

many persons to news of a woman's miscarriage. But they fail to realize that what those struggling with the pain of miscarriage need more than profound words of sympathy is someone to share their grief, a shoulder to cry on.

Society has no death rites for miscarriage.

"Cremated? You want your body cremated after you die?" My husband rolled his eyes and gave me a you-can't-be-serious look.

"All that sending flowers, and buying an expensive casket, and fawning over what a nice job the funeral director did with my hair. What a waste!" I crusaded. "It only serves to glorify death, and we should be affirming life."

Convincing logic. But what I had missed was the real purpose in all those societal traditions surrounding death. They give us communal outlets for our grief, a way to stand together when no one should be alone.

My own mother died at home, with the family around her bed, talking with her, holding her hand. Rather than making her death more difficult, it gave me a head start in accepting her death. I could admit that she was really gone, because I had been with her when she closed her eyes for the last time. That realization laid a necessary foundation for living with her death. All the flowers and food and cards that came gave friends a way to stand with the family. And the socializing before and after the funeral that used to so appall me gave needed chances to talk about her. There was, in fact, something therapeutic in repeatedly rehearsing the details of her death.

In *The Bereaved Parent* author Harriet Schiff recalls the circumstances following her son's death: "In the Jewish faith, following the funeral, we have a seven-day period of intensive mourning called *shiva* during which time prayers are offered and people are encouraged to visit and to bring food to the bereaved family. Our house was nearly always filled, and without question we found this most helpful and therapeutic. When we needed to talk about our son we had many sympathetic ears and they were necessary. While some privacy is essential, being alone with my thoughts after the funeral was the last thing in the world I needed. People were called for and people we got."[6]

Rituals like funerals and periods of visitation are woven into the fabric of every culture, rituals which make the behavior of mourning acceptable and appropriate. But when society refuses to acknowledge miscarriage as a death, a mother's expressions of grief often look bizarre. Said one husband, "My wife spent the day after the miscarriage crying—and the next day, too. When I asked her how long this was going to go on, she exploded in a rage! I wondered if she was going crazy. After all, she wasn't in pain. And after the D and C, the whole illness was over. But she was carrying on like someone had died."

Another young mother told of a woman who had her stillborn child buried in the special section of the cemetery that was reserved for babies. "Every year she'd leave flowers at the baby's grave on the anniversary of his death. Honestly, I felt her behavior was a bit strange and sometimes questioned her stability, to fuss so. I thought it wasn't as if she'd lost one of her children. But now that I've miscarried, I understand . . . and I admire her courage to treat the death for what it really was, even though no one supported her."

Psychologist Edgar Jackson, who specializes in counseling to the dying and bereaved, notes that for a loss to be real it must occur within a context of reality. "A tragic loss that is close to the context of living and real to the emotions causes a sharp but clean wound that can heal itself readily," he continues. "But a loss that is remote and unreal may cause a wound that is infected by doubt and uncertainty. This infected wound tends to heal more slowly and may never heal completely."[7]

When a loved one dies, societal death rites push the death into reality. We see the coffin going into the ground; we respond to the sympathy cards; we return the empty casserole dishes.

But when a child dies in miscarriage, society provides no outlets for the grief. People don't usually sympathize unless the mother has to be hospitalized. There is no body to mourn; no

---

[6]Harriett Schiff, *The Bereaved Parent* (New York: Crown Publishers, 1977), p. 20.
[7]Dr. Edgar Jackson, *When Someone Dies* (Philadelphia: Fortress Press, 1971), p. 10.

headstone is laid. Grief is dammed up in a reservoir with no floodgates to open.

You may be coping with death while in a weakened physical condition.

Perspective on any life crisis is harder to maintain when you don't feel well. And this fact is especially true for women recovering from the physical stress of miscarriage.

Arlene berated herself for not snapping back emotionally from several miscarriages until a friend reminded her of what her body had been through. "If you had had surgeries as close together as those miscarriages have been, you'd expect to be down—and everyone else would expect it, too," she chided Arlene. "But you think that because you can't see any broken bones or stitched-up incisions, your body doesn't need to recuperate. Give yourself a break!"

As a woman mourns for her child, her body may be weak from loss of blood. And even if the miscarriage involved little physical trauma, she may be experiencing the normal hormonal swing that follows when the body is carrying a child one day and is not the next. Some health care professionals estimate eighty percent of the women in post-natal care units show some sign of postpartum depression, usually evidenced by crying and other symptoms. But normal "baby blues" are only compounded when you have no baby there to compensate.

The day I came home from the hospital after our five-month loss, I fell apart emotionally, I didn't want to talk to anyone, didn't want to see anyone, didn't want to live. "Why now," I wondered, "when yesterday I could at least manage to function?" But a dear friend, and the mother of two grown kids, reminded me that on the third day after my daughter's birth I'd fallen apart like this, too. "You'll have sadness ahead," she counseled, "but today's bout is worse just because of baby blues. After Holly was born, you recognized the cause of all these emotions because your milk came in that day. But this time, in the hospital you had that shot to dry up your milk; you've forgotten that to your body, you've just had a baby. Tomorrow, and the next day, will be a little better." And they were.

Postpartum depression may be a more influential factor in the suffering after miscarriage than professionals and mothers alike realize. Besides the commonly held position that the depression can hit within ten days after giving birth, there are authorities who think postpartum depression can stretch from three to six months after giving birth.[8]

If, as many believe, postpartum depression is a biologically induced reality that causes a vulnerability to depression among women with new babies, think of the consequences of these hormonal shifts for a woman who has just lost her child! Perhaps this is part of the reason women find miscarriage so very difficult to handle, and also in part why husbands do not seem to completely share the depth of their wives' sorrow.

The cause of pregnancy loss is often medically vague.

Though there are many possible causes of pregnancy loss, not all are clearly defined. This drives most of us absolutely crazy! As twentieth-century creatures, we're basically cause-and-effect people. For every reaction there has always been an equal-and-opposite action. After all, isn't that what we've been taught? Therefore, we're unprepared to accept the fact that much of the testing for causes of miscarriage as well as some of the treatments are trial-and-error attempts without guarantees. Trial and error is fine for diagnosing the whine in your carburetor or for curing your warts, but when you're dealing with the lives of children-to-be, that can be very unsettling. A miscarriage may be your first

---

[8]Though two thirds of postpartum reactions (often depression) occur within ten days, there may be an increased vulnerability to depression which extends well beyond that ten-day cut off. Studies have shown that new mothers have four to five times the risk of developing psychological illnesses during the first three months after delivery and remain far more "at risk" for psychological disorders for six months after giving birth than women do in general. Simply the stress of new parenting showing? Many researchers don't think so. They attribute at least a part of these giant emotional swings to hormonal changes. For further explanation see *Unfinished Business* by Maggie Scarf (Garden City, New York: Doubleday and Company, Inc., 1980), pp. 279–281.

experience in seeing how very little is known about the human body and how it works. Instead of clear-cut answers to your questions, much of what you get from doctors is murky ambiguities that leave you feeling helpless.

To a mother, a child has been lost.

It was my first visit with Beverly. As we sat in her living room, our three toddlers climbing about and fighting over toys, we made gentle pokes into each other's lives, looking for common ground. The most obvious what-shall-we-talk-about-next topic was her pregnancy. She was at that lumbering, awkward stage just four weeks short of delivery. I groaned inwardly at the thought of the arrival of a third child when her Tina had just turned two and Teresa was barely a year old. I commented on how tired she must be. "Oh," she explained, "we wanted them close together. We're out for a big family. They would have been spaced even more closely, but we lost a baby last March."

She must have noticed my slight stiffening, because she went on hurriedly, "The baby wasn't stillborn—it was just a miscarriage."

Later I thought about Beverly's comments. How matter-of-fact she was as she told me about the miscarriage: "We lost a baby." And then on to grocery-story comparisons. But my conversations with women who have miscarried and my own experience have assured me that it is *never* quite so matter-of-fact. What sadness, what fears, what unanswered questions lay behind that miscarriage confession? I wondered.

And then, as an afterthought, there was Beverly's need to explain that the loss wasn't a stillbirth, as if to let me know I wasn't to feel too badly. It wasn't like losing a "real" baby. It was *just* a miscarriage—almost as if she were apologizing that it hadn't been a more serious loss.

Beverly's apology revealed the fact that she had accepted a myth of mourning which our society holds onto very tightly. It assumes that the more days you've had with a person, the more attached you become; therefore, the harder it is to lose him or her in death. It's the belief in this theory that causes people to say, "How good that the baby didn't live any longer than a few hours, or you could have become so attached." Or "At least you'd only been pregnant three months when you miscarried. Imagine how much harder it would have been to carry to term, and then lose it."

Sometimes this theory holds true; sometimes it doesn't. Of course, the loss of a friend in which you've invested twenty years of yourself will tear the fabric of your heart so that it will never be the same again. But not everyone you've known twenty years has touched you this same way. And haven't there been those you've been with for but a short time, who have so deeply affected your life that the pain of separation from them never quite heals?

So it can be with these babies of ours. Even if your child died so early that his tiny body was barely formed, the loss of who that little one was to you may be mourned deeply, and rightly so. Sociologists Peppers and Knapp agree. "Maternal love, whatever its source, reaches deeply into the very earliest stages of pregnancy and attaches itself firmly to the growing infant," they say. "Loss of that infant is a very real experience, and the mother's grief over that loss can become oppressive."[9]

After her baby's stillbirth, a young mother, wrote:

I Miss Him

I miss him, the babe, the first-born.
In his personality he taught me real joy.
I could not see his laughter or his smile,
But I knew his happiness,
I knew my son, my first-born boy.

I miss him, my dream come true.
All the years of planning,
All the hopes of what and when
He would be came forth in him,
My beautiful boy with his eyes of blue.

I miss him, the one I held that August morn.
No breath could I feel but yet I knew how alive he was.
Memories do not die nor do golden angels.
I'll remember him always,
My babe, my son, my first-born.[10]

---

[9]Peppers and Knapp, p. 29.
[10]Phyllis Adams, unpublished poem, used by permission.

In the same way, you may have become connected to your little one in a deep way, very early in the pregnancy. The changes in your body that began almost at your baby's conception may have become a daily reminder that he or she was there, a new life growing inside you. For some women, the reality of a child's existence hits after they feel movement. And though the emotional rush we call "love" may not come until delivery, for some women that love is every bit as intense toward the growing little one as it will be when the babe snuggles in their arms. This process of bonding between mother and child begins early, earlier for some women than ever realized. So even if a mother's actual days with her child are limited, the loss of that baby can hit as hard as the loss of a much-loved friend.

A pregnancy loss is the death of a part of you.

Experts recognize that during pregnancy, a woman experiences two kinds of changes. There is, of course, the growth of the fetus, but a woman also feels physical and emotional changes within. Losing a pregnancy is the loss of a loved *other*, but it is also the loss of a part of *you*. And these two separate losses, mixed into one, produce a peculiar kind of pain unlike most others.

"I have sorrowed over the deaths of both parents," Myrl reflected, "but there was a different kind of sorrow with losing the babies. It was part of myself dying, and I felt it throughout my whole being."

Others agree. The experience can only be compared to one of losing your sight, your hearing, or one of your legs and knowing that you will never get it back again. Researcher E. P. Furnum observes that with the loss of a loved one, there must be a readjustment in one's self-image. "It is, however," he notes, "altogether different to have to readjust to thinking of oneself as an imperfect human being, a human being that cannot walk or cannot see. That is a pain of a different kind and the feelings that accompany it are emptiness, loss of self-esteem, and feeling low. When a newborn dies, the parents, especially the mother, often describe these sensations."[11]

---

[11]Marshall H. Klaus, M.D., and John H. Kennell, M.D., *Parent-Infant Bonding*, 2nd ed. (St. Louis: C.V. Mosby Co., 1982), p. 262.

Peppers and Knapp concur: "What people do not realize is that for the mother, this infant has been a part of her since conception. She has come to know it in a way that no one else has. In a sense, she has not only lost a child but also a part of herself. Her breasts ache to nurse and her arms long to hold her lost infant. She literally feels empty, weak and insecure; a very real and significant part of her has died."[12]

You had a baby, but you have no memories to cling to.

Parents often report that the death of their baby was worse than the loss of parents or the deaths of older children because the work of grief was so much harder to do. At least with an older child, there are those who knew and loved him or her and years of activities to go back to as a way of keeping the child's memory alive. Pulling out one of the quilts my Grandma Johnston labored over always starts us off on stories about her—like the way she would scowl every time she would see us wearing rollers, "When are you going to get those corncobs out of your hair?" It is the recounting of those memories that makes her life seem real and, in a sense, keeps her alive.

But with a pregnancy loss there are few memories, and the ones that live exist only to the woman and perhaps her husband. "The trauma and tragedy of the deaths of most young people is felt and shared by many people—family, friends, neighbors, school mates, and the community," note Peppers and Knapp. "But what about the death of an infant? What are the reactions of parents, family, and community to the loss of infants? Who is this infant anyway? What is his or her identity? Is this a person to be mourned? There are certainly no community contacts. There are only the mother, the father, and, perhaps, the grandparents who really 'know' the child. Therefore, can the loss of such an individual be so great? So significant?"[13]

If you miscarried, or delivered a stillbirth, you lost a child.

---

[12]Peppers and Knapp, p. 28.
[13]Ibid., p. 15.

And that loss took place in such an abrupt and uniquely difficult way that those who have not experienced it will probably not understand. But your suffering makes sense. You have good reason to hurt.

CHAPTER TWO

Does Everyone Need to Mourn?

As flames licked at the rafters of the barely completed auto-repair shop, the Wilsons huddled together in the pre-dawn cold, watching the blaze that an hour before had been Ned Wilson's livelihood. He tallied his losses aloud as they waited together for a fire truck that would come too late. In addition to the newly purchased building, there was the tow truck, all his tools, the $4,000 lift he had just had delivered. And fourteen-year-old Nancy began to cry.

"Stop it!" her sister ordered. "That's dumb! He'll build another shop. It's nothing to cry about."

With the Wilsons, there was never *anything* worth crying about.

Nancy's sister-in-law died of cancer in her early forties, leaving her husband to care for two daughters he barely knew. But through the entire ordeal, Nancy never saw her brother express any sadness. Even at the grave site, he played the genial host, making small talk and seeing that everyone was taken care of. Nancy stood by, awed by strength that could stare death in the face without flinching. It was then that she decided she would just have to learn to be like the rest of the family. She would have to.

Thirteen years later, Nancy lost her first child in a miscarriage. An ectopic pregnancy, her doctor called it. The fetus implanted in a Fallopian tube instead of in the uterus, so it had to be surgically removed.

"You're very lucky," her doctor told her, peering over the tops of his half-glasses. "If these pregnancies aren't caught in time, the fetus gets large enough to finally rupture the tube. Women have died from the hemorrhaging."

She preferred to think of it as a blessing of God. And there were other blessings, too. For one thing, she and Ryan hadn't officially decided to start a family yet (Ryan was ready; she wasn't), so the pregnancy wasn't really planned anyway. And she had gotten the news she was pregnant just a few days before the ectopic diagnosis, so there had been little time to get emotionally involved. And she had escaped having to agonize over aborting a living being, since the fetus died before surgery. Dr. Hedrick even guaranteed that his repair job on the damaged tube put everything back in good order. "You'll have all the children you want," he promised.

Ryan's boss and his wife sent flowers after the surgery, along with a note telling about their own miscarriage a year before. They warned her to expect an emotional letdown afterward, but Nancy knew there wouldn't be one. "I got off without a scratch," Nancy smiled to herself as she packed to leave the hospital. She was a little proud of the way she had sailed through this first life crisis, strong and composed. Maybe she had picked up more of that Wilson resiliency than she had realized.

Two years later Nancy conceived again, this time by design. The pregnancy test, telling Ryan, and debating about when to inform her new boss was fresh and exciting. And she thanked God for such great timing! Ryan had just left the company he had been with for six years and was consumed with a new career direction, leaving Nancy neglected and a little lonely. The baby would be someone who needed her more than Ryan seemed to right now.

But about eight weeks into the pregnancy, Nancy started spotting. It began inconspicuously, just an intermittent brown staining one quiet Thursday morning. Hardly noticeable. But by Friday the spotting had become a light flow, and she feared something was wrong. Her doctor partnered a busy suburban OB/ GYN practice, so wading through his protective battery of answering services and nurses took perseverance. But when he returned her call, the doctor promised to meet her at the emergency room on Saturday if the bleeding continued. It did, and after an exam he patted Nancy's shoulder as he told her she could expect to pass the fetus soon. Nancy wept a little as Ryan drove her home, but there was little time to cry. They had guests coming in an hour or so, and she needed to start dinner.

About midnight she awoke with cramps pulling at her insides. The spotting turned to bleeding, heavier now, and in clots. Nancy and Ryan didn't know what to expect from a miscarriage. But they decided that since the baby was dead already, they would just ride out whatever came. Nancy lay down on their bed, gripping her stomach, as Ryan stood by helplessly. "Maybe Midol would help," Nancy groaned. "Why don't you go get me some?" She only half believed it would make any difference, but thought going to the Seven-Eleven might give Ryan a way to feel helpful.

Ryan had barely gotten back when Nancy stumbled to the bathroom again, and this time her body pushed out a sizeable clump of tissue. "This is probably it," Ryan said as they stood together looking at the clotted mass in the toilet. "Do you think we ought to save it?"

Together they decided they wouldn't, and Ryan flushed it away as Nancy climbed back into bed.

The next morning Ryan went to church alone, explaining that Nancy "didn't feel well" to those who asked where she was. It hurt her that he hadn't told their friends about the miscarriage. Was he ashamed? she wondered. But Nancy scolded herself for seeking pity. A failure, after all, deserves no sympathy.

Dr. Weiland greeted her cheerily in the examination room Monday morning. He assured her that no, her workouts at the spa hadn't caused the miscarriage. If that were possible, high-school girls who didn't want to be pregnant would jump up and down until they aborted. He smiled, pleased at his ability to interject a bit of humor into these heavy conversations. Miscarriages like hers were common. Most likely it wouldn't happen again. Just one of those things.

Dr. Weiland knew how to keep things in perspective, Nancy thought as she dressed. That was one of the reasons she liked him.

As Nancy left the office, the receptionist stopped her, "Shall we schedule your next appointment?"

"I won't need another . . . I lost the baby yesterday," Nancy answered slowly, surprised at how difficult it was to say the words. The receptionist's eyes dropped, and she mumbled an awkward apology. I will not mention the miscarriage again unless I have to, Nancy resolved. No reason to make others feel so uncomfortable.

Nancy jumped back into her job zealously, determined to divorce herself from the disappointment of the miscarriage as quickly as possible. She was, after all, young and healthy and had a strong faith. God had purposes in everything that touched her, and there was a purpose in this experience, too. She needed to trust that it would work for her good and not ask questions. The few friends who knew about the baby expressed sympathy, but Nancy assured them that it was God's will and she was fine.

In another year she conceived again, and after a textbook pregnancy delivered a beautiful daughter. Meagan's safe arrival gave an indisputable back-up to Nancy's "accentuate the positive to eliminate the negative" theology. Best not to dwell on miscarriage, she advised others. Look at how nicely it had turned out for her. And Nancy cooed to the fragile pink bundle in her arms.

But what Nancy defined as faith lay much closer to what psychologists would call denial. Although she mouthed the words "I lost a child," she refused to let the meaning of those words sink in. True to her Wilson upbringing, any sadness was swept away under a rug of cheerful activity and deliberate control.

Her third miscarriage, however, defied denial.

Nancy blew out the thirty-one candles on her birthday cake, and decided then that another pregnancy needed to be in the offing. Within two months she sat in her doctor's office, urine specimen collected in a baby food jar, sure in her pre-knowledge of the results. She showed all the symptoms already, morning nausea, tender breasts, fatigue. Meagan was going to have a brother or sister. It was nice having experience at being pregnant, knowing what to expect, Nancy mused.

Both she and Ryan anticipated success, but they decided to be careful nonetheless. Nancy rested, ate carefully, watched her weight and kept up her exercise. But despite the precautions, she felt totally exhausted. Prenatal checkups showed no abnormalities, but the tiredness dragged on past its normal third-month cut off. "Maybe it's because I'm older this time," Nancy diagnosed, "or maybe caring for Meagan takes more energy than I realize."

At four-and-a-half months, the weariness was forgotten because Nancy's belly mushroomed. Over a three-week period, she outgrew all her maternity clothes. She made little jokes about expecting a pony instead of a baby, but inwardly she worried. At the Christmas dinner, her two aunts dropped hints about twins, but she shrugged them off. In their eighties, never married, what could they know? She'd see her doctor right after Christmas and get an answer.

"You didn't get all this from eating too much turkey?" Nancy's doctor teased, but his expression betrayed surprise and concern. "Let's do a sonogram and see what's going on in there."

Within ten minutes, Nancy lay on the examination table. She was oblivious to the cold probe moving across her stomach, fascinated as the outline of one, then two tiny bodies appeared on the monitor. She could make out miniature fingers, little toes. "Babies!" she squealed. "Hi, Darlings! This is your mom. I can see you in there!" One lay quiet, most likely asleep, she guessed, and the other twisted and turned and stretched.

Twins! God was giving her two children at once to make up for the two miscarriages before. Then Nancy caught herself, surprised that memories of those miscarriages would resurrect when she thought she had buried them for good.

Ryan was delighted, their friends and family ecstatic. The next few days were full of long distance calls and excited plans for the twosome's arrival. Nancy's back ached, enough that delivery day seemed a long time off. But at least the discomfort was *for* something; they were having twins! She'd rub her protruding stomach and talk to the babies during the long nights she spent awake in the living room recliner, the only place in the house where her sore back could get relief.

Two weeks after the sonogram, Nancy got up feeling badly. "I don't know how I can take care of Meagan today," she complained to Ryan as he ate his breakfast. "I think I'll call Julie to come and get her, and then spend the day in bed." Ryan agreed it was a good idea and kissed her as he headed out the door.

But as she dialed Julie's number, she felt something letting go inside her and then a gush of water between her legs. She didn't have time to even sit before there came another gush, this time mixed with blood. Instinctively she called for an ambulance, and then for her closest neighbor to get Meagan. The thought of her daughter kept her controlled and she waddled to unlock the front door so the ambulance driver could get in, then back to the phone to call Ryan. The rushes of blood were coming every minute or so, and she alternated between worrying about the carpet, and wondering what Meagan would do if she passed out before someone came.

In minutes her neighbor burst in the door, then stopped up short at the sight of the blood. "You'd better get into bed," he gulped, and scooped Meagan into his arms. The emergency team arrived just behind him, and started an IV and oxygen. Ryan screeched up the drive just in time to jump into the back of the ambulance beside her.

Once in the ambulance, she recognized the labor contractions. Finding a familiar sensation in the midst of all the confusion gave her a feeling of control again. Let's see, pant-pant-blow. Wasn't that the routine from her LaMaze class? "It's going to be okay, Ryan," she smiled weakly as she reached for his hand. "God is in charge and this will all work out okay." Why she felt the need to take the role of reassurer she didn't know, but she was pleased at herself for it. By the time they reached the emergency room, she appeared calm, handling the pains, giving her history to the nurses.

But when the babies delivered, one pushing out hard after the other, her composure crumbled. She was losing the two little ones she had seen just two weeks before. But . . . but maybe she wasn't. These were really children! She'd seen them move, even talked to them. Maybe they were big enough to survive this hellish entry into the world.

The doctor let both fetuses plop into a metal pan and started out the door. "Wait!" Nancy pulled at her arm. "Wait . . . if there's anything you can do, any way to save them—we want them given every chance . . ."

The woman looked at her with disgust. "Lady, there is *no* chance. Would you like to see?" And she made a move to shove the bloody contents of the metal pan under Nancy's nose. Nancy felt her resolve collapse, and she turned away toward the wall. How stupid she must look to these people! Struggling to be a valiant champion for an aborted mass of bloody tissue. The doctor ordered an immediate D and C, and an hour and a half later, Nancy awoke, groggy and weak, an IV from the surgery in one arm, and a needle for a blood transfusion in the other. Somewhere in the haze, Ryan asked her about a funeral, but they decided against it. Better just to leave the whole incident behind as quietly as possible.

In a couple of months, Nancy's body regained strength, but her heart was dry and empty. This time she sang no "praise the Lord and press right on" songs. She confessed to Ryan, "I can acknowledge God's right to give or take life as He chooses, but there's no peace in that admission." In another four months she was pregnant again ("I want to get another baby and get this pregnancy business over with."), but a miscarriage followed the conception by eight weeks.

At this fourth loss, Nancy cried. She cried at the onset of mild spotting; she cried through the three days in bed that followed; she cried after the emergency room D and C. She wept over her inability to do what others seemed to accomplish so easily. And she finally wept for these little children whom she would never hold.

So began Nancy's first giving way to the grief she previously had chosen to reject. And as she let go, the stream of tears became a flood of sadness in which she thought she might drown.

For the next year, she was engulfed in unhappiness that refused to be decided away. She pulled back from friends and activities and ministry. She put on weight and for once, didn't care. She read books on midlife crisis, books on spiritual backsliding, books on depression, groping for a way out from under the heaviness. And she wrote journals full of probings into her thoughts, her family, and her life with God, looking for a lifeline in the whirlpool of emotion.

Friends were baffled by the change in her. Even Ryan struggled to understand, with little success. "It's like I'm fighting a legion of demons," Nancy tried to explain, "but I don't even know their names." The humility to admit that she, like anyone else, could be sad and angry and guilty over four miscarriages was slow in coming.

It was a year before Nancy could shed her "always victorious Christian" self-definition enough to write in her journal:

"The return of joy? Maybe it would come if I thanked You, Lord, for the miscarriages.

"But thank You? Something in me stiffens to a resounding NO! In order to thank You, I'd have to believe two things: the losses were allowed by You and that they were for me, good.

"Father, they were *not* good. They hurt. And were disappointing. I felt like I failed. They were humiliating. Nothing good came of them! I was poked and prodded and scraped. And I came away more tired and empty, older and fatter.

"And allowed by You? Please—I'd rather think they had nothing to do with You. They were just a sad fluke of life; my particular body doesn't do well at holding onto babies. It's simply a genetic fact, something You weren't even a part of. If I involve You, you see, then I'll need to ask why it all happened. If You are only good, why would You allow experiences with so much ugliness? No, I'd prefer to acknowledge that they happened, give the children I conceived up to Your care (as I have), and leave it at that. Some things in life are sad, and we just get through them as best we can."

But then she wrote, "It sounds so good. But what do I do about Your instruction to 'give thanks in all circumstances, for this is God's will for you in Christ Jesus'?"[1]

The process of emptying out the anger and sadness had begun. And to her emptiness, God began to reply. The healing she needed didn't come that day, but it did come, and later Nancy would write,

"Lord, these miscarriages *were* allowed by You and for my good. It's just that the good of them is on a much grander, eternal

---

[1] 1 Thess. 5:18.

scale than what I can grasp. I've been insisting that You prove to me a short-range, comfortable, material kind of good before I'll accept the losses.

"Thank You for the miscarriages. I accept them and thank You that in Your eternal goodness You allowed them for my best, for the babies' best, for Ryan's best, and for the sake of others we will touch."

"I see now," Nancy reflected, "that I was afraid of grief, of losing control. And in my understanding of faith, grief simply wasn't an option. I now believe that 'the valley of the shadow of death' is a passage that must be traveled. There are no detours. But I did find at the end of the valley, not an abyss, as I feared, but a doorway into a deeper life with God."

The consequences of not grieving.

In their study of mothers and mourning, Larry Peppers and Ronald Knapp often saw the consequences of a grief denied, especially in the case of miscarriage.

"Grief may be openly expressed, or it may remain hidden and unexpressed in feelings of guilt, bitterness, and sadness. The overt expression of grief can be highly beneficial to the person who has experienced a loss. Hidden grief, on the other hand, may remain unresolved; furthermore, it can be detrimental to the physical, mental, and social well-being of the grieving individual."[2]

That may be a sound perspective, but it is difficult to swallow, especially when the pain comes from losing a child. Perhaps the courage to face reality begins when we realize there is really no alternative.

Labor in the delivery of my second child was labor indeed. There were times, I'll admit, that once those heavy contractions hit, I wondered how in the world we'd ever been talked into this "natural childbirth" idea. What happened to the romantic picture of me and my Coach smiling tenderly into one another's eyes as he held my hand and we sailed through the delivery? Just

---

[2]Peppers and Knapp, p. 27.

as they wheeled me into the delivery room, a huge contraction hit, and I let out an enormous whoop, equal in intensity to what felt like a two-ton vise being screwed down on my abdomen. On the next gigantic contraction, I yelled again. I looked at my doctor, a bit embarrassed. "Honestly," I confessed, "I have never hollered like that in my entire life." And we both laughed. But his nurse cleared her throat. "Honey," she reprimanded, "you might get more done if you took the energy you're using to make so much noise and used it instead to push this baby out."

Correction given; correction received. There was no more yelling from me, and in three more contractions, the baby was out. It was simply a matter of channeling the energy productively rather than wasting it to no purpose, and in the process, prolonging the pain.

If grief is refused a natural outlet, it chooses an unnatural and more destructive way to express itself. The question is not whether or not you will choose to mourn, but whether or not you allow yourself a constructive way to mourn. And if you cut off natural outlets for mourning, the sadness will take its toll in other ways, sometimes on your body.

In a book for funeral directors, author Edward Martin warns about "frozen grief," the term for repressed or blocked sadness. He calls it the most dramatic of the abnormal bereavement reactions. "Blocked from normal emotional outlet, it [grief] sometimes erupts within the body, finding indirect expression in a physical disease. The intestinal tract, which seems to be the weakest link in the body's defenses against emotional assaults, is hit hardest and most often."[3] He cites a study in one large hospital which showed seventy-five percent of the cases of ulcer of the colon to be associated with grief situations. Sometimes these physical symptoms appear within a short time after the loved one's death; sometimes not for years.

Why don't we grieve?

Some, like Nancy, are too proud. Grief means admitting weakness, and that may be very difficult to do.

---

[3]Edward Martin, *Psychology of a Funeral Service* (Grand Junction, Colorado: Colorado Printing Company, 1977), p. 113.

Others are afraid to mourn. If you allow yourself to really admit the loss, you may fear that the pain of that loss will consume you.

And if you are a Christian, you may reason that grief is equated with unspirituality and unbelief. You do, after all, base your life on a belief that death is only a short passageway into life that goes on forever. Perhaps to you, mourning constitutes an outright denial of that belief.

For Christians only: on the validity of mourning.

I caught just enough of the radio speaker's thoughts on grieving to come away with this particular gem: "A trembling lower lip may be more the sign of a true Christian than a stiff upper lip." And I realize now how much that man understood of a godly perspective on grieving.

Jesus Christ was not ashamed to grieve.

John the Baptist was dead, his life lost in a gory and degrading capitulation to the sadistic whims of a bitter woman and her seductive daughter, who had called for his head on a platter. The news horrified and sickened Jesus' disciples. Such a tragic end for one of whom Jesus had said, "A prophet? Yes, I tell you, and more than a prophet. . . . Among those born of women there has not risen anyone greater than John the Baptist."[4]

But the death meant something more to Jesus. John was His second cousin, a personal link to His earthly beginnings. Jesus, no doubt, had grown up hearing over and over again the story of the precious and prophetic three months their mothers had spent together before either of the boys were born.

Now John was dead. John, the one to publicly proclaim Jesus to be the Lamb of God, come to take away the world's sin. John, the one who had given himself, even before seeing the miracles of Jesus, to cry in the wilderness, "Prepare the way of the Lord!" Others believed Christ and spoke up for Him, but there could

---

[4]Matt. 11:9b, 11a.

not be another like John, committed to Him from even before the day a voice from heaven would sound, "You are my Son, whom I love."

And what a time for John to die! Jesus had just received a disappointing rejection from His home-town folk who heard Him and snorted, "Isn't this the carpenter's son? Isn't his mother's name Mary, and aren't his brothers James, Joseph, Simon and Judas? Aren't all his sisters with us? Where then did this man get all these things?"[5] This was no time to lose a close friend!

But Jesus, of course, was God incarnate, the King of Glory, the Conqueror of death and Author of life eternal. And He knew full well that John at that moment revelled, alive and whole, in the glories of heaven and all the wonder of the God the Father unveiled. So how did He respond to John's death? Did He give a ringing reminder of the truth of the resurrection?

On the contrary. "When Jesus heard what had happened, He withdrew by boat privately to a solitary place."[6]

He went out, alone, to embrace the weight of His painful loss at John's death. The God-man was acknowledging the void left in His life by the death of His friend. He was strong enough to look the pain of separation in the face and let it wound Him.

Later, His friend Lazarus would die. And in the account preceding Lazarus' resurrection, Jesus would again affirm mourning as an appropriate response to death. When He heard of His friend's illness, Jesus came to Bethany not to console his sisters but with the stated purpose of raising Lazarus from the dead. "Our friend Lazarus has fallen asleep; but I am going there to wake him up. . . . So then He told them plainly, 'Lazarus is dead.' "[7]

Jesus did not set out for Bethany to simply be with Mary and Martha at their time of need or to sentimentalize over death. He was not the weak-kneed victim, cowering helplessly in the face of an undefeatable enemy. He came to reverse this particular instance of death and by the reversal to glorify himself and show His Father's power.

---

[5]Matt. 13:55, 56.
[6]Matt. 14:13a.
[7]John 11:11b, 14a.

But at the sight of the brokenness of Mary and her companions, Jesus wept.

Perhaps the tears were angry tears. The account says He was deeply moved in spirit and troubled. He could not have been troubled by His own helplessness, for He would startle His friends with His power in only a few moments' time. But He may have been angry at the pain death brings, with the rage that only a mourner can understand. Angry, perhaps, at death itself. Angry enough to cry. And there came no heavenly rebuke for His tears, no accusations of unspirituality or intimations of unbelief. Jesus was feeling the human sorrow of death, and God the Father approved.

Somehow we've taken the scriptural promises of peace and comfort and victory to mean the absence of pain. Author Joyce Landorf remembers how that after learning of the death of her newborn son, God's presence came rushing in, comforting, sustaining, upholding. But she also confesses, "I did not write of the hours [of anger] that followed later because I felt guilty about them. I did not know that being angry over your loss was normal or that the anger would pass. I could not write of those angry thoughts then because I thought Christians were not to have them."[8]

The Old Testament reveals a grieving God. "I wail over Moab," He says, "for all Moab I cry out, I moan for the men of Kir Hareseth. I weep for you."[9] And in the New Testament, God the Son bares His heartbreak at the loss of those He loves: "O Jerusalem, Jerusalem, you who kill the prophets and stone those sent to you, how often I have longed to gather your children together, as a hen gathers her chicks under her wings, but you were not willing!"[10] He mourned the children He loved. He expects you will mourn the loss of yours.

I don't want to romanticize grieving. Real mourning is ugly and deep and wrenching, no matter how flowery and tasteful sympathy cards try to make it out to be. But trying to sidestep

---

[8]Joyce Landorf, *Mourning Song* (Old Tappan, New Jersey: Fleming H. Revell Company, 1974), p. 58.
[9]Jer. 48:31, 32a.
[10]Luke 13:34.

grief represents a proud and silly effort to avoid the unavoidable. When Jesus promised that those who mourn would be comforted, He laid down an inescapable prerequisite for receiving the deep, rich wonder of God's healing.[11] To become a candidate for His comfort, you first must open yourself up to the pain of mourning. If you are a Christian, you share the life of One called "a man of sorrows, and acquainted with grief."[12] Can you choose to be otherwise?

Do not mourn as those with no hope.

Paul admonished the Christians at Thessalonica, "Brothers, we do not want you to . . . grieve like the rest of men, who have no hope."[13] Paul told his fellow believers not to grieve hopelessly, but he did not challenge them to forego grieving.

Grief *is* different for a follower of Christ. Even in the depths of sorrow, hope breathes. Hope that you will see your child again in heaven. Hope in God's capacity to infuse suffering with purpose. And hope that because of His healing power, your sorrow will not go on forever.

---

[11]Matt. 5:4.
[12]Isa. 53:3.
[13]1 Thess. 4:13.

CHAPTER THREE

A Grief in Process

In the Iowa farming community where I grew up, 4-H was a natural part of the rhythm of life. In the summer, time was not marked by weeks or months, but by its relationship to one of the fairs. June and the first three weeks of July were Before-County-Fair-Time; the first two weeks of August were designated After-County-Fair-but-Before-State-Fair-Time.

One particular year, we had a project for the fair worth being excited about. My older brother had become somewhat of an apprentice to a farmer in the area who specialized in raising purebred Hampshire sheep. Through that connection, the sheep we had to show had good chances of being prizewinners—maybe even champions. And champions in each class went on to the state fair. That, of course, would give an excuse to hang around Des Moines all week and to sleep in the 4-H dormitory. All very grown-up stuff.

A week before the fair, we culled the select sheep from the flock and penned them up on the yard to keep them cleaner and see that they didn't get too much exercise. One morning, one of our normally tame dogs went wild, invaded the sheep pen, and killed three of those prize lambs. We were as shocked and horrified as only adolescents could be. My sister and I cried, and my oldest brother grabbed his .22 and shot both dogs on sight.

For my brother Charlie, however, there was no crying, stomping, or shouting. When I looked out at the pen later, I realized that he had quietly removed the dead sheep and replaced them with three others.

Each of us finds his own way to work through sadness.

There is no set mold, no "right" way, for mourning a loss. One counselor advises, "Grieving involves physical, mental, financial, and interpersonal pain. Not all who grieve will experience all these aspects. Nor do we experience them in an orderly fashion necessarily. Also we do not experience them 'once and for all' and move steadily up—or down!—the rungs of the ladder, as it were. The grief experience is more like riding a roller coaster, unpredictable, sometimes scary, and once you're on, you can't get off until the end of the ride."[1]

But finding your own way to grieve may not be as easy as it sounds. For most of us, it is unfamiliar territory. And picking your way through new terrain is usually slow and full of mistakes. Barbara, hospitalized after a miscarriage, longed for a resident, or a nurse, or a social worker, someone to tell her how much of her anguish was "normal."

And her longing was justified. Though the journey is left to each individual, a roadmap can ease the way. There are common feelings among those who grieve—feelings like denial, fear, anger, guilt, and loneliness. Understanding them can make grief less overwhelming.

Initial reactions.

My neighbor, Bill, died suddenly of a heart attack while driving home from his daughter's house. In my naiveté, I marveled at his wife's composure during the funeral. How amazing that she could do so well in the face of losing the man who had been her reason for living the last forty years, I marveled.

Now I know that her careful composure would not—could not—last if Florence was to truly recover from Bill's death and be able to make any semblance of a life afterward. What I was seeing was a woman in shock, a normal, God-given response to

---

[1]Mildred Tengbom, *Help for Bereaved Parents* (St. Louis: Concordia Publishing House, 1981), p. 13.

loss. It's as if all her senses were dulled for a time to allow a breathing space before she would need to marshal her resources and face the terrible reality ahead. Shock was also God's gift to Nancy as she hemorrhaged in miscarriage. If the fact that she was losing the twins had become a reality right then, she might never have been able to call the ambulance and take care of her child. The protection of shock may have saved her.

Denial is another form of shock. It is the feeling that this loss is not real, and nothing bad has happened. My five-year-old fell and broke her arm quite badly in two places. As we raced to the emergency room, she looked down at her wrist, now a crooked S-shape, and said, "Mom, I know this is just a dream. I know I'm going to wake up and my arm will be all straight." And I thought at once of how my friend had used those same words as she talked about her divorce. Ron and Laurie had been married eighteen years and in the pastorate for most of those years. A model home, a model family. Then Ron announced that he no longer loved Laurie, no longer wanted her or the kids, and was leaving. And Laurie was left with three teen-age children and a broken life. She wrote me a few months afterward, "I wake up in the morning and think, 'This *cannot* be happening to me.' "

Acknowledging the loss.

Denying the loss is a normal reaction. But it must be a temporary reaction if healing is to come. Moving through denial to an acknowledgment of the loss is particularly difficult in miscarriage. No baby, no funeral, no pictures, no memories of the child. It's as if the baby never was, and therefore there is no loss.

Having a body to view may be much more crucial to the resolution of grief than we realize.

Some adoption agencies encourage unwed mothers not to see their newborns before releasing them for adoption. But a California psychiatrist who counsels these mothers found that the mothers who *did* see their babies did much better afterward. They worked through their feelings more quickly and later wanted to marry and have children they could keep. "The basic relationship between mother and child is so deep and intense that its reality cannot be denied without hazard," he explained.

Dr. Edgar Jackson applies the same truth to coping with death. "Psychiatrists have said that the moment of truth that comes when the living persons face the dead body can be one of the most significant and therapeutically useful parts of the process of coping with death. Until the whole person is willing to face the facts of the change that death brings, it is difficult or impossible to begin the true work of mourning. . . . Unpleasant and painful as it often is to face reality head-on, the choice you have is simple and unavoidable. You either face reality and release yourself from the hold of denial or you go on living with self-deception. As long as you persist in the denials and delusions you are unable to do the work of mourning. And unless you can do the work of mourning you will build your life upon illusory attitudes that cannot stand up as you move into new and demanding situations."[2]

Remember when Jill insisted on seeing the tiny fetus she had just miscarried? Little did she know that in her natural curiosity she was instinctively following the quickest path to genuine healing.

But others, like John and Charlotte, have not been so lucky. Their son died in utero five months into the pregnancy, but after the induced labor and delivery, they never saw him. John remembers, "They said the decision was ours to make, but I sensed we'd really have to insist if we wanted to see the baby. And I didn't have what it took to insist on anything at that point." Charlotte, too, has regrets. "We both feel that our sorrow lasted much longer than it needed to because we had such a difficult time connecting to the reality of what had happened."

Perhaps like Charlotte, you never saw your baby. Or, perhaps your experience was like Martha's, whose only sighting of her little one was a vague, sketchy outline drawn on a sonogram screen. Martha spent the next thirty days in a nightmarish limbo— a few days of bleeding, then none. She'd go back to work optimistically telling others things were looking better, only to be

---

[2]Jackson, p. 12.

home in bed again two days later, wondering how to answer the queries about whether or not she was losing the baby. A month of agony later, the sonogram traced only an empty fetal sac. "And really, though there was a lot of bleeding," Martha said, "I never passed any sizeable amount of tissue I could have identified as the baby." She had carried a child, and lost a child. But she had nothing to hang her sadness on.

Tangible reminders.

There came a time in Nancy Wilson's personal confrontation with her miscarriages when she knew she needed something tangible to help acknowledge their reality. Enough repression. She uncased her Smith-Corona and pecked out requests for her medical records to her doctors and the hospitals in which she had been cared for during each of the losses. What came back in those brown manila envelopes was painful to read. "Those records unearthed feelings I'd carefully denied," she said, "and I wouldn't want to read them again for a long time. But just seeing those forms with 'Patient: Nancy Wilson; Condition: Spontaneous Abortion' typed out again and again was like forcing myself to look into the coffin, a tangible way of facing the fact that my children had died. Now I've found more positive ways to remember my children, particularly through sharing with other hurting mothers the comfort God has given me. But reading those records was, for me, a necessary starting point for admitting what had really happened."

After you've faced your loss, you may need to create a quiet memorial of your own, something tangible and physical to mark your child's existence. Or you may find you have a special memorial already at hand, like the diary Andrea had written during her pregnancy. Six months after her son's stillbirth, she confided, "If our house had been on fire and I could have saved only one thing, I'd have grabbed that diary and run!"

If you had begun collecting baby things and working on a nursery, don't be too quick to empty everything out. You may want to keep a special blanket or a couple items of clothing. I held onto a little baby outfit a friend in Chicago had sent when she heard I was pregnant—one of those incredible finds she knew I'd just have to have. It was a starched white sailor suit, complete with rows of black piping, gold buttons, and a bright red, properly square-knotted tie. And stenciled across the chest with exacting military regimentation, were the words, "Name, Rank, Cereal Number." Of course with my last name being "Rank," and the fact that both our husbands were ex-Navy men, it was perfect with a capital *P*.

Having a tangible reminder of your child's existence may not matter to you. What is important, however, is that you face your loss squarely, because such an acknowledgment marks the beginning of healing.

The period of suffering.

The initial shock and disbelief of the miscarriage is behind you. It *has* happened; you can't escape it. Your child was growing within you; now that child is gone. What follows is the pain of grieving that must be worked through on the way to recovery and healing. There are many forms this suffering may take; they differ for each person. But most who've suffered the grief of a loss like this will tell you about feelings of fear, failure and help-lessness, guilt, a strong sense of isolation, and of anger.

Fear.

In the aftermath of a miscarriage, you may find yourself with fears you never entertained before. The first day at home after my third miscarriage, a neighbor graciously called to ask if she could keep my two-year-old for the day so I could rest. But I couldn't let Holly leave. And I asked Mike not to go anywhere either. I feared that if they left, they might not come back. I felt embarrassed owning up to these feelings, since I've always con-sidered myself more brave and independent than the average person. But fear gripped me too intensely to be decided away. So Mike and Holly stayed.

The intensity of these fears subsided with time. But even now, years later, as I tuck my little ones into bed, the thought occasionally crosses my mind that they might not be alive in the morning. This realization does not paralyze me, nor does it curtail normal living. But since the miscarriages, life has become a much more fragile commodity, not to be taken for granted. Ever.

Fears can sometimes sublimate themselves into parts of life that have nothing to do with childbearing or pregnancy. During the course of my last miscarriages, several friends became interested in the survivalism movement. They began storing up dried food, hiding away bags of silver coins, and debating the merits of leaving the city to live off the land. This sort of doom-looms-ahead mentality has never appealed to me, but in the emotional disorientation of grief, preparing for coming catastrophe made a lot of sense. I had never expected pregnancy losses, yet they happened. If that could happen, my subconscious reasoned, so could anything else. So I began writing to dried food companies to compare prices and bought a three years' supply of razor blades (certainly to be in short supply when the economy crashes, our friends assured us). I read books about the coming economic disaster and worried with these friends over protecting our children during anarchy.

The world economy did not collapse (though it still may—who's to say?). But now I handle this prospect without it dominating my thoughts or life decisions.

Fear is often a sister of grief—fear of another pregnancy, fear of not being able to have more children, fear for your health or the safety of those you love. You may experience all of these fears as you grieve for your lost child.

Failure and helplessness.

In the book *Coping with Miscarriage*, Christine Palinski describes her feelings after her miscarriage:

"For me, the disappointment and anger remained after I left the hospital—later they were joined by a host of other unpleasant emotions. There was no transition period. A few hours earlier I had been carrying a baby, doing what I wanted to do and winning everyone's approval. Now, suddenly, I was reduced, cut down. I had become a source of disappointment to myself, to Mark, my family and friends, and others. For probably the first time in my life I felt like a loser. Before I had been fortunate enough to get what I went after. Maybe I had adjusted my goals to fit my potential for success; I had not met with failure in anything that mattered. This surely was failure. A very personal, direct kind of failure. There was no one else to tie it to—the pregnancy was mine, in my body, and it didn't work!

"By the time of the second miscarriage my self-image was fully involved. This new consciousness of failure in combination with other people's reactions was rapidly changing how I felt about myself. I began thinking of myself as unfortunate, powerless—or at least, less powerful. The strongest response I found myself eliciting from others was one of pity. That was devastating to one who was accustomed to responses at the other end of the spectrum.

"I disliked the pity reaction, but wasn't able to redirect it in other people, so I started responding to it. My earlier confidence was eroding, especially in my own body. I found myself in a strange mind-body conflict; I distrusted my body, its signals, its abilities. Since a large part of my concept of myself was naturally tied to my body, that was debilitating to my whole person."[3]

Numerous times after our unsuccessful pregnancies I'd moan to my husband, "How *can* this be so difficult? Teen-agers have babies all the time—without even wanting to! What is wrong with me?"

For some women, there remains after miscarriage the sense of having failed not only themselves, their husbands and friends, but also their babies. Explained Lisa, "What job is more central to mothering than to protect your child? Mine couldn't even make it to birth."

Harriett Schiff writes of her own bout with sagging self-esteem: "When the feeling of powerlessness sets in, we find ourselves in the sorry situation of having to deal not only with our bereavement but also with our inability to have prevented it. Powerlessness is one of the true quagmires of grief that we will

---

[3]Hank Pizer and Christine Palinski, *Coping with a Miscarriage* (New York: New American Library, 1981), p. 109.

encounter and one of the most painful stages in coming to terms with grief. It is awful to bereaved parents to realize that nothing they can do or say can change the finality of their child's death. One of the basic things taken away from a bereaved parent is the conviction of possessing the ability to control, to have some say, in this world."[4]

Guilt.

"Guilt became a major theme for me," said one woman. And another, "I stumbled around in my guilt." Women who miscarry often hold these sorts of remembrances of their experiences. Getting accurate medical information can sometimes help to allay guilt, but the feelings of guilt are hard to shake with a situation like miscarriage because so little is medically certain.

An entry in my journal revealed how I struggled with the burden of guilt for my miscarriages:

"Lord, again, about the miscarriages . . . I may have caused them. Those little ones may have failed to enter the world because of me.

"Before the third loss, I went on that strict diet. I really lost weight (could even get into Margie's size nine jumpsuit!). But I refused to increase my eating, even after I knew I was pregnant. Did I value a skinny body above the lives of those babies?

"With that same pregnancy, we changed doctors and signed up for that one-day-in-the-hospital plan at the clinic to save money. I was treated by a student. We didn't have maternity insurance, I rationalized, and our money was so tight. But, Lord, perhaps if I had stayed with Dr. Williams or had gone to a specialist, as Sally suggested, they might have known what to look for, and the baby might have lived. Was I too cheap to care for my kids? We could have found a way to get the money—there is always a way.

"And when our college friends called about visiting for a few days, I didn't say no, even though I'd started spotting. The doctor had said 'bed rest,' but I baby-sat for their children on a 100-

[4]Schiff, p. 55.

degree August day while they went sightseeing. Was I crazy?

"Lord Jesus, if, in the objectivity and all-knowingness of heaven, You know that I did cause some or all of these miscarriages, please forgive me. I'm so sorry (though that sounds so shallow at the taking of a human life). But if I did cause the end of a life You created, Jesus, please forgive me."

You may find that upcroppings of guilt can plague you for months after a pregnancy loss. Several years after our losses, I can see how unwarranted most of my guilt was. There's no medical evidence to suggest that a different diet, or a more expensive doctor, or additional rest would have saved the pregnancies. But guilt is grief's devoted tagalong. Even if you've done *nothing* wrong, grief invariably insists that you *must* have. One woman miscarried, she told me, because she drank diet pop. Another felt remorse over an antibiotic she took (even though she had none of the medicine for a full year before her pregnancy). You can expect to feel guilt as you grieve.

Isolation.

If you feel very much alone in this experience of grief, it may be because you are.

Many of those around you will not think of miscarriage as the loss of a child. They see it as "an unfortunate experience," to be sure, but expect you to be your old self again just as soon as your body is stronger. When after three months, six months, a year or more has passed and memories of the miscarriage may still be as tender as an open wound, people probably won't understand. "It wasn't, after all, like a real baby," they may say to one another. "And she can have others. She really should have snapped out of it by now." Experiencing a normal grief in a culture that hides from death will appear strange to some people and will no doubt bring with it a sense of isolation.

And there may be depths to your grief that even your husband will not share. Sociologists guess that this is due in part to the almost immediate physiological changes which pregnancy brings to a woman's body. These changes result in a solid enough bond between mother and child even before birth that miscarriage brings a painful rending of that bond. Since there is no similar physical change for the man, he is often unable to experience the depth of his wife's grief.

After Barbara's miscarriage her husband planned a vacation to California to help take her mind off the loss. But the trip proved to be nothing but an on-going quarrel between them.

Finally they came to understand their separate perspectives. Arnie could feel the disappointment and the need to make new plans. But there was an intensely personal part of the miscarriage, like an amputation, that Barbara could describe but not really share with Arnie. Both realized that they had lost something important, but most of the loss would be Barbara's to endure.

Anger.

At the death of her one-day-old son, Joyce Landorf burst out, "You say, 'but just think—David is with the Lord!' My mother-self rises up and screams out with inescapable anger, 'Well, you tell the Lord to give him back to me. I want him in my arms, not God's.' "[5]

A father recalls his anger when he learned his son was dying. "I remember weeping. I remember also the fury and frustration at my helplessness and the unfairness of it all. 'Why?' I asked the nun who tried to bring words of comfort. 'Why this child who has a lifetime of living yet to do? If we must give up a child, why not our retarded younger son who will always need supervision?' "

" 'God must love you very much,' Sister Annemarie gently replied while my anger boiled over, 'to ask so much of you.' "

" 'Love like that I can do without.' "[6]

The anger is there, seeking a target on which to land. I spent a lot of time angry at doctors and the medical establishment. Why hadn't they given me more information? Spent more time with me to chart a course of tests and treatment? Cared more?

Other women are angry at their spouses for how they did or

---

[5]Landorf, p. 62.

[6]Gerald Oosterveen, "Memories of My Son," *Focus on the Family* (January 1984), p. 10.

did not give support. Or at friends for things that were said. Or mad at other mothers who sail through complication-free pregnancies to birth healthy, perfect babies. Or mad at their bodies for letting them down. Or mad at a hundred daily little things that never used to bother them.

Some who are honest enough to admit it are even angry at God.

"You have the power over life and death," we want to shout heavenward. "You could have protected our babies, yet You didn't."

Of all grieving responses, I believe that anger is the most difficult to accept, particularly for those of us who are Christians and particularly when we're angry with God.

A few years ago a woman from our church was diagnosed as having cancer. Lucy was barely thirty, the mother of three small children. During the agonizing months of radiation and chemotherapy that preceded her death, many of the reports that filtered back to us were not positive. "She's taking it so poorly," the word was whispered. "Now she's mad at the doctors. And she shuts her husband out sometimes." We were all very disappointed. Lucy was, after all, a Christian. Where was the valiant cry of death swallowed up in victory? We tsk-tsked inwardly, and prayed that she'd get straightened out.

Today I shudder as I think of my reactions. I see how insecure I am over my first gray hairs and smile wrinkles around my eyes that won't go away when I stop smiling. Then I think of Lucy, watching all of her hair fall out from radiation treatments, trying to deal with a body nauseous, swollen and full of pain. Dying. And I was *surprised* she drew back from her husband? I was *disappointed* at Lucy's anger?

Psychologist Paul Tournier observes, "Open the Bible: Moses, Job, the authors of the psalms, the prophets—there is plenty of righteous anger there. Jesus Himself overturning the tables of the money-changers in the Temple. . . . Holy Writ is full of conflicts, conflicts between men, and between God and men, and when true harmony—the harmony of faith—supervenes, it is only after an explosion of anger. In the personal history of many believers a holy rebellion has been the first step towards a trusting encounter with God."[7]

For a long time my anger took the form of its sister expression: depression. Mike and I took the Taylor-Johnson Temperament Analysis Test during the period of my pregnancy losses. I wanted to take the test because I'd been so overwhelmed with a vague feeling of unhappiness; I hoped that the test results might give some insight. The results were, however, an enigma to me. I didn't profile as depressed at all, but instead terribly angry. In fact, I rated in the ninety-eighth percentile on the anger chart. That really made *me* angry! My problem wasn't anger—it was depression! What was wrong with that dumb test anyway?

I've since learned that most psychologists define depression as anger turned inward. At that point in my experience, being angry with God was absolutely not acceptable. Being guilty and depressed were. So subconsciously I had chosen what I felt was the lesser of the two cosmic evils. "Say you're not angry, and you won't be. Say you've accepted your losses without a whimper, and you will." Or so I believed. It appeared to work, except for that "down" feeling I simply couldn't shake.

Physical symptoms of grief.

Crying is not the only outlet our bodies choose for grief.

Grief can feel like a lump the size of a grapefruit in your throat that makes it hard to swallow and speak. You may lose your appetite or begin eating too much in a vain effort to fill the void in your body with food. You may feel more tired and lethargic than you have ever felt in your life. Or you may feel restless and unable to sleep. You may experience heart palpitations or nausea. Or you may have trouble breathing, like a friend whose fiancée had just deserted him. Between sentences he would let out the deepest, body-wresting sighs I have ever heard. It was as if he were reaching to the very depths of himself and trying to push out the sadness.

When a Des Moines *Register* reporter asked the woman whose

---

[7]Paul Tournier, *Creative Suffering* (San Francisco: Harper and Row, 1981), p. 85.

ten-year-old son had been kidnapped a year before and was still missing how she was feeling, she answered, "There's a hurt around my heart."

"It described just how I felt about our miscarriage," Jill noted. "There was a heaviness, a real, physical ache around my heart that wouldn't go away."

During the period of sadness after my miscarriages, I was absolutely convinced I had hypoglycemia (low blood sugar). No one in my family had a history of any diseases related to blood sugar. But every time I read the list of symptoms for that disease, I identified with nearly every one: intense weariness, an inability to concentrate, difficulty in making decisions, depression. A day in a laboratory waiting room and six blood draws later showed no signs of hypoglycemia. What I thought were concrete signs of hypoglycemia were really manifestations of grief.

For months after John and Charlotte lost their baby, both showed symptoms of various illnesses. "Now we see," Charlotte reflected, "that we simply had physical symptoms of grief. As some of the sadness resolved, so did the sickness. It's just that we didn't know grief could affect your body, too."

The period of recovery.

It takes time.

Someone has said that when mourning is involved, healing can be spelled T-I-M-E. You will not wake up one bright morning with all your feelings of guilt and anger and aloneness miraculously lifted.

Because in the last few years we've heard much talk about the stages of grief, you may feel there is an orderly progression of feelings through which you must pass to live with your loss. Not so! Even after you feel yourself on the other side of your grief, there may still be times that the pain will come back to surprise you.

When the brother of Christian author and speaker Evelyn Christenson died, this great woman of prayer clung to God's promise that He would work all things together for good, even an untimely death. But with her characteristic honesty, she admitted, "But my loss at my brother's death still jumps up at me in unexpected places—a plane stopover in Detroit, for instance. While Bud was living, every time a flight I was on made a stop in Detroit, I would get off, dash into the terminal and call him on the phone just inside the gates. The first time I came into that airport after he died, my feet dragged into the waiting room. A great void swept over my whole being. My stomach did a peculiar flip-flop as I shuddered inside. Just last month while I was being driven to the Detroit airport following seminars, a vaguely familiar sight flashed past the car window. It was the fire department which housed the emergency squad Mother had summoned to try to resuscitate Bud. And there it was again. The loss welling up, unheralded, inside me."[8]

A mother interviewed for a television documentary said she had what she called "David attacks" for years after the death of her little boy. The major work of mourning was behind her, but there would be times—family holidays, the anniversary of his death or his birth—that would open the wound again. "But," she noted, "the 'attacks' are fewer, and less intense as time passes."

Some authorities advise parents to expect that it will be a year or more after the death of a child before the worst passes. A pregnancy-loss support network known as The Compassionate Friends advises bereaved parents to avoid making major moves, such as changing houses or jobs for at least a year. There is no escaping the fact that healing simply takes time.

The need to let go.

There will come a time when you will need to choose to let go of your grief, and this choice may be more difficult than it sounds. For some women, the feelings of sorrow are the only tie they have to their child, and they feel that when those are gone, the memory of the child will be lost forever. Others feel guilty as their joy and vitality begins to return. There can be, incredibly,

---

[8]Evelyn Christenson, *Gaining Through Losing* (Wheaton, Illinois: Victor Books, 1980), p. 73.

the temptation to hang onto grief even after the work of grief is over.

But you will not, you cannot, lose the memory of your baby. You won't forget. Instead, you will find that you have made your baby's life a part of your own in a way that will leave you richer.

Kathe McDaniel described her recovery after the loss of her little son in this way: "I seemed to go on for a long time in a dark tunnel. Sometimes fighting it, but more often letting myself be carried further and further down. Most of the time I just felt numb—I began to wonder if I were still alive.

"One day, to my surprise, I realized I had smiled—at a flower, or a bird, or a child laughing. No, I thought, it can't be. How can I smile without my child? And my guilt would drive me back into that dark pit again.

"Then at lunch one busy day I realized I hadn't thought about the emptiness all morning. That dull ache was not the first thought in my mind upon awakening. When I stopped to think about it, I realized there had been other days and times when I had lived through a few hours without the pain. Another afternoon I actually laughed out loud at a funny story my neighbor told me. I was coming back to life. The pain went away more and more often and for longer periods of time. When the emptiness did return it was sharp, but not so intense as before—not so all-consuming. I continued to live and grow and love. Slowly my life came back to me again. My feelings and hopes and dreams came back; my laughter and enthusiasm returned. Slowly but surely I became a whole person again."[9]

A *whole person* again. . . ! However feeble it may seem to you at the moment, that is a glimmer of hope for the future.

[9]Kathe McDaniel, "Then . . . Now . . .," *Compassionate Friends Newsletter*, 3:4, Fall, 1980. Used by permission.

SECTION TWO:
FINDING OUT WHY

CHAPTER FOUR

Questions Only You Can Answer

Some women, especially those who have only miscarried once in a first trimester loss, don't ask many whys. They find out that pregnancy loss is relatively common, and that, like lightning, it generally doesn't strike twice in the same place, and that's all they need or want to know about miscarriage.

"My first miscarriage didn't get me down," Becky recalled. "I was busy, healthy, twenty-three. I felt I could try again a hundred times if I wanted to. After all, I wasn't successful the first time I tried to ride a horse either. But after my second loss at twenty-eight, everything looked so different. I felt pressured by the fact that those years to try weren't unlimited after all, and even if they were, this second loss seemed so much, well . . . sadder. I needed reassurances I didn't seek before."

Let's assume Becky is seeing a new doctor. Where will treatment begin? Under most circumstances, Becky can expect to start off with a wonderful test, wonderful because it's cheap, simple, painless, has no negative side effects, and can sometimes produce immediate results. This wonder test is called "Ask the Patient," otherwise known as, The Medical History.

You have much helpful information to give your doctor, much more than you know. If pregnancy loss was a one-cause, one-cure kind of ailment, your medical history wouldn't matter as much. But as you know all too well, such is not the case. So first your doctor will need to know about *you*.

Your doctor's questions may come in various shapes and sizes,

but the major areas of interest will be:
1. How many pregnancies have you lost?
2. How far along in the pregnancy were you with each loss?
3. Did you have any illnesses while pregnant?
4. What did you do for birth control before the loss?
5. How old are you?
6. What is your family medical history?
7. Could there have been contributing factors in your life-style?

If you understand these questions and are ready to give informative answers, you may be able to take yourself a long way toward some whys for your loss, with nary a drop of your blood sent off to the lab for testing . . . at least, not yet.

How many pregnancies have you lost?

A fairly straightforward question, right? But you may need to think about your answer.

Perhaps you missed a menstrual period or began exhibiting signs of pregnancy. Your doctor's office told you to wait for another missed period before coming in, so they could be assured of conclusive results on your pregnancy test. But before your appointment came around, you began flowing, perhaps more heavily than usual, and with heavier clotting. You assumed the pregnancy was a false alarm. It might have been. But there is also the possibility that you had, indeed, conceived but lost the pregnancy at a very early point. More and more physicians are beginning to agree that this is often the case.[1]

In a lecture at the University of Iowa Medical School, Dr.

---

[1]A study done on the Fallopian tubes and uterine cavities of a group of women undergoing elective hysterectomy showed eight embryos which hadn't implanted yet and twenty-six implanted embryos (fourteen days old or less). Of these at least twelve of the embryos were so abnormal that they either could not have implanted in the uterus, or if they had implanted their continued growth appeared nearly impossible. These findings indicate two things: that pregnancy loss is probably much more common than ever dreamed; and that many of the losses, particularly first-trimester losses, are caused by genetic error. See A. T. Hertig, "The Implantation of Human Embryo. Histiogenesis of Some Aspects of Spontaneous Abortion," in J. Behrman and R. Kistner, eds., *Progress in Infertility*, 2nd ed. (Boston: Little, Brown and Company, 1975).

Roger Williamson explained that when physicians talk in terms of fifteen to twenty percent of pregnancies miscarrying, they are referring to what he calls "clinically recognized pregnancies," those in which a pregnancy test has proved a woman is pregnant. These documented losses would involve embryos at least four weeks old or older, of course, because it takes that much time to miss a menstrual period and get an accurate reading on a pregnancy test. But earlier losses he calls "preclinical abortions," meaning pregnancies that no one could validate yet were lost. Dr. Williamson explains, "Fertilization usually occurs in the Fallopian tube, and by the sixth day of life the embryo has implanted in the endometrium. At this time the pregnancy cannot be recognized clinically and will continue to be unrecognized for one and possibly two additional weeks. Therefore, loss of an embryo prior to about three weeks embryonic life will probably not come to medical attention."[2]

My doctor guessed I had two of these very early losses. My period had been two to three weeks late; I'd begun to feel pregnant (tender breasts, tiredness, nausea). When the "period" finally came, the flow was heavier than usual with lots of clotted-looking tissue passed. And these abnormalities happened to a lady who has *never* been late for a menstrual period for *any* reason. My menstrual cycles have weathered major life catastrophes without missing a beat.

This new perspective on early losses might cause you to take a second look at your menstrual history before you decide you miscarried just once.

How far along in the pregnancy were you?

Knowing the timing of the loss can help your doctor eliminate some possible causes and spotlight others. Myrl's repeated pregnancy losses always came after the first trimester, and three of them happened after twenty weeks of pregnancy. Information like this would alert most physicians to the fact that genetic test-

---

[2]Roger A. Williamson, M.D., "Genetics of Spontaneous Abortion," unpublished paper.

ing would be a waste of time for Myrl and Bob, since later pregnancy losses are rarely caused by genetic abnormalities in the fetus.

Losses before twelve to sixteen weeks.

Three of four pregnancy losses happen during the first trimester. And if yours did, you'll be encouraged to know that most of these losses are caused by genetic errors. Of these, the majority are simply *random* errors that won't happen again. Data collected at the University of Iowa and other places indicate that in ninety to ninety-eight percent of the cases, the losses were the result of a *chance* something went wrong with the baby as it was developing. Genetic testing only shows a problem in the parents two to ten percent of the time. Thomas H. Green, in his widely used medical text, says, "These pregnancies were destined to fail at the very outset and the process of abortion [miscarriage] simply represents the natural termination of an unproductive enterprise."[3]

Losses beyond sixteen weeks.

If your losses came in the second trimester, or later, your doctor will wonder about a variety of possibilities.

Were there malformities in your uterus? Many of these abnormalities are ones for which you can be tested. The next chapter deals with this subject in more depth.

Or your doctor may ask if you showed signs of toxemia, a kind of blood poisoning with symptoms like high blood pressure, protein in your urine, and swelling in your hands and feet.

Or perhaps there were problems with the placenta. Childbirth educators warn about getting help at once for vaginal bleeding because they know that bleeding can mean that the placenta is loosening from the uterine wall too early, and the results might be fatal to the baby. And other things can go wrong with the placenta. Sometimes the placenta attaches low in the uterus, in-

---

[3]Thomas H. Green, Jr., *Gynecology—Essentials of Clinical Practice*, 3rd ed. (Boston: Little, Brown and Company, 1977), p. 297.

stead of in its usual position, which can cause serious problems. In other cases the placenta either doesn't grow normally or doesn't function properly, causing a decreased oxygen supply to the fetus. Or there can be either an overabundance or an inadequate supply of the amniotic fluid.

If you simply delivered for no apparent reason, your doctor will wonder if your cervix was what the medical community has termed "incompetent," unable to stay closed under the weight of a growing baby.

The timing of your pregnancy loss may give your doctor clues as to why it happened.

Did you have any illnesses during the pregnancy?

Did you have any viruses, like rubella, herpes, or hepatitis while pregnant? Did you take any drugs or medications? Several anti-convulsant drugs routinely given to epileptics, like Dilatin, have a bad history in relation to miscarriage, yet women taking them are not always warned about this side effect.

What did you use for birth control before the loss?

In the last decade, the birth control pill turned out to be much less magic than many of us were led to believe it was going to be. It not only prevents ovulation, but affects nearly every organ in the body. If taken during a pregnancy, or even two or three weeks before conception, it can cause abnormalities in the baby's limbs and other birth defects. Therefore, of course, it would be suspect as a factor in pregnancy loss. That's why most doctors encourage a few months' delay between getting off the Pill and a try at conception.

If you became pregnant with an IUD (intrauterine device) in place, there may be questions about whether or not it contributed to the loss. An IUD causes inflammation in the uterus, so doctors guess it makes the uterine lining less receptive to a fertilized ovum implanting, and thus it keeps a pregnancy from succeeding. (Some say the IUD works a bit differently. Though they admit it causes inflammation, they also think it causes spasms in the Fallopian tubes which keep the sperm from fertilizing an egg.) Either way, the picture would not be an encouraging one for a pregnancy begun in the presence of an IUD. Although some of these conceptions have gone to term, IUD pregnancies often either miscarry or begin growing in the Fallopian tube in a very dangerous condition known as ectopic pregnancy.

Even if the IUD had been removed by the time you conceived, IUD users report three to five times more frequent occurrences of Pelvic Inflammatory Disease, an infection of the uterus and tubes that can hinder a pregnancy in ways we'll discuss in the next chapter.[4]

How old are you?

Biologically speaking, the optimum age for having babies lies somewhere between twenty-two and twenty-six. Women over thirty-five show increased possibilities of miscarriage for a variety of reasons. For one thing, a woman is born with all the eggs she will ever have, so naturally these eggs age as her body does, and this aging may affect the future chances of a fetus's survival. More mistakes occur in the chromosomal distribution during cell division among older women. And older women have more variances in their hormonal levels. Endometriosis, a disease affecting fertility, gets worse with age. And older women show an increased incidence of benign fibroid tumors in the uterus.

One study showed a twelve percent miscarriage rate for twenty-two-year-olds, a twenty-two percent rate for women aged thirty-six, and a jump to forty-one percent of women aged forty-two who miscarried. The rate of loss was nearly three-and-a-half times as high for women over forty as their twenty-year-old counterparts.[5]

Of course an over-thirty-five tag doesn't mean you are destined to miscarry. My mother was thirty-six when I was born and

---

[4]For an excellent, and much more thorough discussion of birth control alternatives and their impact on fertility, see "Contraception and Conception" in *What To Do When You Think You Can't Have a Baby,* by Karol White (Garden City, New York: Doubleday and Company, Inc., 1981).

[5]Pizer and Palinski, p. 15.

thirty-eight when my sister arrived to finish out our tribe of six. But increased age can be a factor in pregnancy loss, so that is why your age will matter to your doctor.

Those who say increased age is no longer a problem in child-bearing are often referring to the use of a test known as amniocentesis. You have likely heard of it as a way to check for genetic abnormalities and problems like Down's syndrome in unborn babies. During the test, a four-inch-long needle goes in through the abdomen into the amniotic sac, and fluid is taken out to test for abnormalities. But this test only shows the presence of abnormalities; it cannot fix them. Sometimes women over thirty-five are encouraged to try a pregnancy, with the assurance that if the child is not normal, amniocentesis will let them know so they can abort the baby. But of course for the woman who wouldn't consider an abortion, this particular test would hold little value.

We haven't come as far as it might seem in helping the older woman who wants to have a baby. But many of us would rather know there are risks, and face them head-on.

What is your family medical history?

Robin's mother had one miscarriage and then lost a baby two days after his premature birth at seven months. While pregnant with Robin, she threatened to miscarry again and was given the dangerous drug we call DES, a synthetic estrogen we now know causes cancer and other cervical and vaginal problems in the unborn children exposed to it. All these facts would give a physician avenues to pursue with Robin that might be fruitless with others.

Is there a history of pregnancy loss or newborn death in your family? Does anyone in your family have disorders like cystic fibrosis that are possibly inherited? Are there factors in your parents' health that might have influenced these losses? Your physician will want answers to such questions.

What is your lifestyle like?

Do you smoke? Or drink alcoholic beverages? What are your eating habits? Are there any opportunities in your living or work situation for exposure to dangerous chemicals or potentially hazardous X-rays?

Have you ever had an elective abortion? Studies in Japan and England showed a three- to nine-fold increase in miscarriage among women who had had previous abortions. And women who have had *repeat* abortions are particularly at risk for later pregnancy losses. Says author Karol White, "The devastating effects of abortion are summed up by a British Perinatal Mortality Study, which showed that a past history of abortion increases the neonatal mortality rate by fifty percent."[6]

It is important that you keep these questions in perspective. When your doctor asks about your eating habits, for instance, don't assume that you caused your miscarriage because you weren't faithful in taking your prenatal vitamins. We all know women, like my neighbor, who survive for nine months on Oreos and Pepsi and still produce children. Your doctor is looking for the extremes. Dr. Barbara Batts, a Kansas City gynecologist, reassured me that the kinds of poor eating habits that result in miscarriage consist of severe malnutrition, probably a malnutrition I would never see in a lifetime.

If these lifestyle factors don't always result in pregnancy loss, then why does your doctor ask about them at all? Because in most cases, studies of either humans or animals have shown these things to cause *increased risk* of miscarriage. And if all the other probing into whys for your loss turn up nothing, but you smoke heavily, then there might be good reason to question whether cigarettes are a factor in your pregnancy loss.

All this questioning is a valuable investment of your time and energy. Your answers, though not conclusive evidence, may eliminate some possible reasons for your miscarriage and reveal others. And in contrast to some of the tests discussed next, these verbal probings cost nothing and take little time. Your answers will help you and your doctor decide which of the other tests might be valuable for you. Perhaps several will; perhaps none will. But if you are under the care of a pro, he or she will look first to what *your history* reveals before sending you off for a battery of lab tests.

---

[6]White, p. 101.

CHAPTER FIVE

Questions That Tests Will Help You Answer

Now that you have told your doctor about your medical background, chances are that you're about to hear that favorite one-liner, "Why don't we run some tests?"

Not every physician follows the same route in the pursuit of an answer to why a pregnancy loss occurred. This field of study is a mass of changing information, with new studies, new techniques daily coming to light. Some treatments once considered a good bet are now in question; others are being reinforced.

There is no standard operating procedure in looking for the cause of pregnancy loss. But armed with an overview of the areas most specialists pursue, you will be able to ask good questions and get satisfactory answers about the purpose of various tests.

Most physicians will use six questions as guides for their testing decisions:

1. Are there any abnormalities in your general health?
2. Do you have any infections?
3. What is the physical condition of your uterus?
4. How "normal" are your progesterone levels?
5. Could you be having an "immune" reaction to your fetus because of blood group differences?
6. Do either you or your husband have any transferable genetic problems?

How is your general health?

When he or she asks about your health, your doctor probably isn't interested in whether or not you jog every day. Of greater concern is whether there are severe malfunctions in the major systems of your body, malfunctions that might create a hostile environment for the developing baby. One of the symptoms of lupus, for example, is repeated pregnancy loss. Severe problems with the thyroid, kidneys, high blood pressure, and diabetes have all been investigated for their connection to pregnancy loss.

The tests doctors order to screen for these diseases consist of relatively routine blood tests—a CBC (complete blood count) and a blood chemistry profile—which check the function of nearly every body organ. Sometimes a thyroid study (called a T-4) is ordered to look for low thyroid.

Do not begin to fret that the minor bladder infection you had last summer might have caused your miscarriage. Or that because you lost a baby, maybe you have some disease which has thus far gone unnoticed.

The kinds of diseases that could affect pregnancy loss are generally those that women are aware of anyway. Dr. Charles King of the University of Kansas Medical Center says that it is very rare to find undetected diabetes, for instance, as the reason for a pregnancy loss. The other effects of a disease as serious as diabetes are usually obvious and severe enough that a woman would know she had such a condition well before a miscarriage.

The tide of medical opinion comes and goes, too, about whether or not these illnesses actually do connect to pregnancy loss in any significant way. But since the tests for them are relatively simple (just a blood draw) and inexpensive, until all the facts are in, a check is probably warranted.

Do you have any infections?

Your doctor may order a cervical culture (done much like your yearly pap smear) to look for various infections. One called T-mycoplasma, for example, has been found in the tissues of aborted fetuses but not in full-term babies, so there could be a link between the infection and miscarriage. Also, couples with a history of infertility and frequent miscarriages have a greater number of positive T-mycoplasma tests than the average population. And in a Boston study, thirty-six infertile women treated with an antibiotic showed no apparent medical reason for their infertility except that all had positive T-mycoplasma cultures. And after the women and their husbands were treated for the infection, 84 percent of the couples reported a pregnancy within a year.[1] This finding does not constitute a major medical breakthrough, however, inasmuch as the organism has also been found in women with no history of reproductive problems.

But even though more questions than answers exist about the effect of T-mycoplasma, if a culture shows that it is present, the treatment with tetracycline is simple, inexpensive, and one with few side effects. (The treatment, however, must be done before fertilization takes place.)

Another example of an organism doctors look for is a parasite carried by cats (serum toxoplasma) that has been shown to cause pregnancy loss. One reason pregnant women are warned not to change kitty litter is due to the danger of contracting this parasite.

What is the physical condition of your uterus?

A Johns Hopkins Hospital study of women with a condition known as "double uterus" determined that only one of four had serious reproductive problems as a consequence. The other seventy-five percent showed no ill effects.[2] Only one in seven hundred women have some unusual formation of the uterus or vagina, and many of them go on to bear children.

Sadly, some don't.

Problems with the structure of the uterus might physically prevent either the implantation of the embryo in the uterine wall or carrying the pregnancy to term. The uterus can have two

---

[1] *T-mycoplasma: Its Role in Infertility and Miscarriage* (Belmont, Mass.: Resolve, Inc., 1980).
[2] J. Pritchard and J. MacDonald, *Williams Obstetrics,* 15th ed. (New York: Appleton-Century-Crofts, 1976), p. 493.

chambers instead of the usual one or an irregular shape (a Y-shaped "forked" uterus). Or there might be large fibroid tumors or adhesions on the uterine wall.

Sometimes the Fallopian tubes can be blocked by scar tissue so the fertilized egg can not properly implant in the uterus and begins to grow instead in the tube itself. This very dangerous condition, now the number one cause of maternal death, is known as ectopic pregnancy.[3]

The danger of ectopic pregnancies comes from the fact that they are often hard to detect in time. When the implanted embryo outgrows its home in the Fallopian tube, as it must, the tube ruptures and internal bleeding results. This rupturing often occurs by five or six weeks into the pregnancy, before the woman may know for sure that she is pregnant. Or she may have discovered the pregnancy but be showing only some vaginal bleeding, so that a threatened miscarriage may be suspected. More severe symptoms, and much more dangerous symptoms, include abdominal or shoulder pain (from a build-up of blood in the abdomen after the tube ruptures). Immediate surgery to remove the ovum and to repair or remove the ruptured tube is an absolute necessity.

There are several causes of ectopic pregnancy. Scar tissue in the Fallopian tubes can result from endometriosis, a condition in which the endometrial tissue (the normal lining of the uterus) can be found outside the uterine cavity. Forty percent of women with endometriosis will have some degree of infertility.

And some ectopic pregnancies come about in the aftermath of infections like gonorrhea, which cause pelvic inflammatory disease (PID). The infection hits the Fallopian tubes and, though antibiotics may clear up the infection, the tubes are often left scarred; this scarring invites ectopic pregnancy.

Scarring in the tubes can have other causes, as well, so don't assume venereal disease if your friend tells you she had an ectopic pregnancy. Surgery to repair the Fallopian tubes can leave scarring, and sometimes the tubes are simply malformed so that the fertilized egg cannot travel down them. Furthermore, as

---

[3]Molly McKaughan, "The Ectopic Epidemic," *Woman's Day* (April 3, 1984), p. 62.

mentioned earlier, IUDs have also been suspect as a contributing factor in ectopic pregnancies.

One of my losses was ectopic and the cause never determined. I skipped a period, but a few weeks later started a brown spotting that didn't quit after the usual four to five days. A pregnancy test came up negative, but still the bleeding continued. The doctor guessed an ectopic and ordered what he called a laparoscopy. He made a small incision just under my navel, and inserted a small telescope-like device into my abdominal cavity to see if there was a pregnancy and, if so, where it was located. In the surgery that followed, the ovum was removed and the tube sewed up. An X-ray a year later showed the tube open and functional.

I was more fortunate than many women. For some, the ruptured tube cannot be salvaged, so their chances for another conception are cut in half. And statistics show that after one ectopic pregnancy, a woman has a thirty-three percent or more chance of having a second, especially if whatever damaged the first tube (pelvic inflammatory disease, for instance) could have damaged the other tube as well.

Many uterine structural problems can be diagnosed with the help of a hysterosalpingogram. Fortunately, the name is worse than the test. It is an X-ray of the uterus, using a dye which is injected into the cervix and flows through the Fallopian tubes. I still remember the fascination of watching the screen while that chalky dye squirted out into my uterus. "Ha!" I thought to myself, "I really must *have* a uterus. There it is outlined in living green-on-black." At any rate, I found the test interesting and reassuring.

Some of the scarring, tubal malformities and other uterine problems are being treated surgically. And new techniques involving microsurgery and lasers have opened up possibilities of pregnancy for women who thought there were none. And there will be more help coming; consumer demand is on your side. One of six couples who wants to have a baby cannot. And since problem pregnancies happen most often to women in their thirties and forties and more women are having their children during those years, the need for such treatments will only increase.

An incompetent cervix is the last category of structural problems we will explore. If your pregnancy loss came late in the second trimester and you simply delivered with no cramping and little bleeding, it could be that your cervix was not strong enough to take the weight of the growing baby. You are not usually born with this malady. Rather, the cervix weakens from a particularly difficult previous delivery or perhaps from a poorly done cervical biopsy.

But such a problem can often be treated. During a future pregnancy, either a band or stitches can be put around the cervix to keep it closed. The work is done somewhere between the fourteenth and twentieth weeks of pregnancy, and then the patchwork removed just before delivery.

How "normal" are your hormone levels?

I laugh every time I hear the words "normal" and "hormones" used together. The majority of my interactions with hormones have left me feeling anything but normal—just ask my husband five days before my period begins!

But those of us eager to bear children talk about hormones like progesterone with a tinge of respect because it appears that our progesterone levels matter so much in this quest to have children. Here's why.

After you ovulate, progesterone exerts a massive effect on your body. Before ovulation your body is producing only two or three milligrams of progesterone a day. After ovulation, progesterone levels shoot up to some twenty or thirty milligrams a day—ten times what they were just days before. And it is progesterone that acts directly on the lining of the uterus to make it more spongy and lush, ready to nourish a fertilized egg when it implants. (If the egg isn't fertilized, of course, this lining sloughs off and your menstrual period results.) Without this dramatic rise in progesterone levels at the right time, the uterine lining does not prepare to receive the fertilized egg as it should, so implantation and growth are impossible.

How do you determine if your progesterone production is normal? Physicians usually ask you to do the chart-your-temperature exercise (Basal Body Temperature is the official name) for two or three months. Why? Progesterone is heat-producing, so your temperature should rise as the progesterone levels in your body rise. But if you tend to show low temperature increases or late ones, your doctor may suspect a hormonal abnormality and ask for a blood serum level progesterone to be drawn four to eleven days prior to the next period. Some physicians prefer an endometrial biopsy of tissue from the upper uterine level taken two to three days before menstruation. (In this procedure, a small portion of the lining of the uterus is removed and checked.) This may be more accurate, but certainly is not as convenient for the woman as a simple blood test.

If progesterone levels are low, the obvious treatment would be to add more. Right? For a while physicians thought so. Adding progesterone seemed like a magic answer for many miscarriages. Doctors prescribed it in the face of threatened miscarriage, hoping it would turn the tide. But treatment with added progesterone has not proved especially effective. One medical text claims no improvement in pregnancy success by adding progesterone. And now some wonder whether low progesterone levels actually cause miscarriage or whether they are just the effect of another, yet unknown, cause. Maybe doctors have been treating a symptom instead of the real problem.

Doctors who do prescribe progesterone are careful to see that it is natural progesterone. Synthetic forms of the hormone are not FDA approved because they appear to result in a higher incidence of birth defects. Because natural progesterone is poorly absorbed by the body, rectal or vaginal suppositories are most usually prescribed.

In a variation of this hormone-levels approach, Clomid or HCG (human chorionic gonadotropic) is given to stimulate ovulation and consequently increase progesterone production.

If your doctor talks in terms of hormone therapy, he or she will likely do so with some caution, and rightly so. Not much is known about the long-term effects on the mother or the unborn baby of these higher levels of hormones artificially introduced to the body. So, at present, hormone treatments probably stir up more questions than answers.

My experience with hormone therapy provides a classic illustration of why it is wise to ask questions about the treatment program your doctor prescribes. One of the physicians who treated me used progesterone routinely with habitual aborters. About the same time I was under that doctor's care, I heard a doctor on a TV talk show recommend progesterone as a real hope for women who had trouble completing pregnancies. But another OB I checked with was appalled at the idea of such a casual use of a hormone for which, he told me, the success rate had been poor and possible dangers to the fetus had not been determined. Last year a gynecologist told me she rarely used progesterone, and a specialist agreed, noting that he used it in only ten to fifteen percent of the cases he treated.

Could you be having an immune reaction to your growing fetus because of blood group differences?

You've had German measles; you're now exempt from having German measles again. Why? Credit goes to your body's ability to protect itself from substances that it thinks will harm it. These protective devices your body produces are called antibodies. And when the German measles virus invaded your body, you reacted by developing particular antibodies to fight off that virus if it ever appeared again.

When you get your toddler *immunized* against diphtheria or tetanus, you're once again taking advantage of this wonderful feature of self-preservation. The nurse injects a small amount of the virus itself into your child and his body fights back with those antibodies. If ever he were to confront an honest-to-goodness case of diphtheria, his now built-in protection would keep him safe. What a system!

But physicians are now wondering if this same system of developing immunities comes into play in a negative way when certain incompatabilities exist in the blood groups of a mother and the child she has conceived. Perhaps when the fetus inherits his or her father's blood group, and that group has certain incompatabilities with the mother's, the mother's body sees the fetus as a foreign invader and rejects it.

A recent account of a Kuwaiti woman who had had fourteen

miscarriages in ten years noted that her problem stemmed from the presence of a rare antibody in the blood called anti-P. Each time the woman became pregnant, these anti-P antibodies mistakenly regarded the baby's cells as foreign and attacked them.[4]

This idea of blood systems opposing each other is not new, of course. You know that everyone's blood is not the same—you may be type A, for example; your husband type O. And the incompatability of these particular blood groupings is the reason you can't receive a blood transfusion from or give one to just anybody. And in some cases, these blood type differences can cause trouble in pregnancy.

When someone asks if your blood is "positive" or "negative," the question refers to your Rh factor. Eighty-five percent of the white populace, and ninety-five percent of blacks, have a positive Rh factor; the others are Rh negative. This particular difference in blood types has been proved to have significant bearing on those of us trying to have children. In a situation where a mother is Rh negative and the father Rh positive, the child who is conceived may wind up with his father's Rh positive blood, and it is likely that some of the baby's Rh positive blood cells may enter the mother's bloodstream, particularly during delivery. Since these blood cells are foreign to her body, she will fight them off by producing antibodies against them. And once the antibodies are there, they are there to stay.

There will likely be no problems for this first baby. Usually that child is born safely before the mother's body can manufacture enough antibodies to do him or her any harm. But trouble usually comes during a second pregnancy, if once again the baby has Rh positive blood. During the pregnancy, some of the antibodies from the mother's body may cross the placenta to the baby and begin destroying some of the child's red blood cells. The baby becomes a high risk for anemia, jaundice, brain damage, and death. Author and speaker Joyce Landorf lost a baby to Rh disease; he died of internal hemorrhaging shortly after birth.

In 1968, the vaccine Rh immune globulin became available

---

[4]"Woman Gives Birth after Fourteen Miscarriages," *The Des Moines Register* (February 26, 1984).

to combat this destructive disease. Before the vaccine was in wide usage, an estimated forty thousand babies were born each year with Rh disease. Now the number has dropped to approximately seven thousand. And even those cases could have been prevented if the mothers had had the needed vaccination. The shot must be given to the mother within seventy-two hours after delivery of her first child, to protect future babies from trouble.

Understanding the implications of Rh blood differences can help you understand if your doctor wants to test you and your husband for other blood group differences. Besides the ABO and Rh systems, there are at least forty or fifty other blood group substances. These may cause antibody formation in the mother just as the Rh differences do, so some of these antibodies may affect pregnancy loss.

If your doctor does find some of these differences, treatment is aimed at preventing you from becoming sensitized initially. Or if you do already have the antibodies formed, your doctor will work toward minimizing fetal difficulties in the same way Rh babies are helped. You may have heard of post-delivery, or even intra-uterine, blood transfusions to try to save the lives of babies caught in this Rh-factor struggle for life.

It is not important that you become an expert in blood chemistry. What is important is that if your doctor suggests testing for blood group differences in you and your husband, you understand why.

Do either you or your husband have any transferable genetic problem?

The possibility always exists that you miscarried because of a genetic defect you or your husband carry and you passed on to the baby. These types of defects can be detected from a simple blood sample from you. When my husband and I were searching for reasons for my miscarriages, the idea of genetic testing appealed to me. It seemed to offer, in the midst of this sea of ambiguities, a kind of black and whiteness I longed for. Either my chromosomes measured up, or they didn't. And if they didn't, maybe doctors would say we could never have children. Disappointing though that news would be, there were times when I would have traded the disappointment for a forced exit from this trying-to-have-babies merry-go-round.

But it is unlikely that the test will come up with anything. Of those first trimester miscarriages attributed to genetic abnormalities, probably less than five percent are due to the parents' chromosomes. The rest are chance happenings. And testing for genetic abnormalities, though simple for you, is expensive and rarely gives answers to the why of miscarriage. Unless you have reason to suspect genetic problems—for instance, because one of your siblings has a birth defect like cleft palate or a genetic disorder like cystic fibrosis—this test will probably be done only after most every other possibility has been explored.

Should you bother with all this testing?

Maybe, maybe not. Your doctor will be able to give you some idea of what might and might not be worthwhile from your history.

And money is certainly a factor for many couples. When I asked counselors from the Regional Genetic Consultation Service of Iowa what all of this testing would cost, they handed me a very simple, but helpful sheet with the following facts about some common procedures—what they cost and how often they actually point to a cause for pregnancy loss. Percentages were determined from a study of women who had had three or more pregnancy losses before the fourteenth week of pregnancy.

Test	Cost	% of time results show abnormalities
T4 (thyroid)	$18	Low
CBC (blood chemistry)	$46	Low
Cervical culture	$30	Low
Hysterosalpingogram	$75	10–12%
Hormonal evaluation	$50	8–10%
Chromosomes for both parents	$865.50	3–7%

In the end, the testing decision is yours. How much do you

need to know to put aside the past and answer your questions about future pregnancies? The problem with any testing is the lack of guarantees it offers. You may go through the whole process—and explore other options, as well—and still not find out the answers you are looking for. But if you do go into the experience well-informed about the options, you can later rest in the satisfaction that you did what was right for you.

CHAPTER SIX

Now for Your Questions

1. *Does bleeding always mean you are going to miscarry?*

No. Somewhere between twenty and fifty percent of all pregnant women have some bleeding, yet only half of them go on to miscarry. One OB even reports a patient who bled enough to need transfusions and still delivered a healthy baby. There are various causes for bleeding, one of which can be the implantation of the embryo in the wall of the uterus.

If you will possibly miscarry, there are other signs your doctor will look for that tell much more than the bleeding does. Is there a heartbeat? Is the cervix beginning to dilate? Have you passed any tissue? He or she may call for a very sensitive test that measures the level of the hormone HCG in your urine or blood. If the level of HCG has dropped from earlier in the pregnancy, it may mean that the fetal placenta is not functioning anymore and that the baby has died. If your pregnancy is more than five weeks along, the doctor may order ultrasound to see if an embryonic sac and a fetus are present. Naturally in very early losses, ultrasound would be useless, since the fertilized ovum is not even visible until at least five weeks.

2. *What exactly happens in a test with ultrasound?*

Ultrasound (sometimes called a sonogram) uses high-energy sound to give a picture of the inside of the uterus and of its contents. A technician slowly moves a probe over your abdominal area, and as the sound waves bump up against the mass of the placenta and fetus, you'll see a drawing of the goings-on inside the uterus on the machine's monitor.

Doctors rely on ultrasound to help determine things like the baby's age, placement in the uterus, the presence of twins, and the positioning of the baby before delivery if there seems to be a question of a breech birth. It is a painless test and at this point considered safe, though some question its liberal use, since so little is known about the long-term effects of passing these sound waves through the body of a developing fetus.

3. *Does bed rest prevent miscarriage?*

One specialist says, "I think the tremendous emphasis that's placed upon bedrest is really a carry-over from older days when we didn't have anything else to offer the patient. In most circumstances it won't cause any problems, but it also probably doesn't do a lot of good. But I doubt that there are very many ladies who actually continue a pregnancy because they have had bed rest. Admittedly a patient who goes to bed may have a miscarriage tomorrow afternoon rather than this evening, but it is probably not going to affect the outcome of the pregnancy in very many situations, except, perhaps, in a later pregnancy problem like an incompetent cervix."[1]

Unhappily, even though bedrest may have been prescribed in earlier days because the doctor had little else to offer, today's medical options are not much better. Most physicians will agree that after you've begun spotting, there's not much they can do but wait. So if your doctor advises bedrest, you certainly won't be harming your pregnancy by doing as he or she says. But there's no guarantee resting will save a threatened pregnancy. One doctor said, "I see women who harbor tremendous guilt after a loss because they didn't rest. But for many of them, bedrest was simply impossible. They had other children to care for, or life demands which simply couldn't be shelved. It helps them to know that bedrest is no cure-all, and that chances are good it might not have made a difference."

4. *Does everyone need a D and C after miscarriage?*

No. The purpose of a D and C (*dilation* of the cervix and

[1]Dr. Charles R. King, from a June 23, 1983 interview.

curretage, or scraping, of the uterus) is usually to be sure all the tissue has been expelled from the uterus, because tissue left behind can cause excessive bleeding or infection. But in miscarriages prior to five or six weeks of pregnancy, and sometimes later, all of the tissue often passes by itself; the fetus and placenta usually are expelled together. After that time period, they more often expel separately because the placenta has had a chance to more firmly attach to the uterine wall. Therefore, a D and C may be necessary to ensure that no tissue remains behind.

After a loss at eight weeks, my doctor asked me to make note of how long spotting continued. If spotting or cramping lasted more than a few days, or if it didn't seem to lessen, I was to schedule a D and C. In my case, however, that proved unnecessary.

5. *My doctor told me to save the tissue I passed for examination. Why?*

"There are two or three bits of information that are useful," one expert stated. "One, if the patient does not bring any tissue in and a D and C is not done, there may be a question as to whether or not the patient was pregnant or whether she simply had an abnormal menstrual period. Second, careful pathologic examination of the tissue may provide evidence for the reason of the pregnancy loss. Birth defects could be identified, abnormalities with the placenta, some types of infection could all be identified."

Don't feel, however, that if you didn't save the tissue, you have forfeited your only chance to find out why the pregnancy failed. It is not often that any conclusive evidence comes from these tissue exams. Sometimes the doctor sees the tissue just to be sure it has all been expelled, to help in the decision about whether or not to do a D and C.

6. *How long after the miscarriage should we wait to begin having sex again?*

Most physicians will advise that you wait until all bleeding has stopped, the cervix is closed, and if you had any stitches, they are healed. Usually two or three weeks is sufficient. You'll want to remember, though, that ninety percent of women begin menstrual periods just four to six weeks after their loss, so you will want to plan for some kind of birth control precaution.

7. *When I first found out I was pregnant, I was very disappointed. We hadn't wanted a third baby. Then a month later, I lost the pregnancy. Could my attitude have influenced the outcome?*

Dr. King, associate professor of OB/GYN at the University of Kansas Medical Center, responds, "I think there really is no scientific evidence of emotional difficulties or stress as a cause for pregnancy loss. Imagine a sixteen-year-old girl, a high school cheerleader, queen of the homecoming dance, who is pregnant. If there's a stressful situation, that's it. If it's really true that stress and emotion can cause pregnancy loss, then a young lady in that situation should be able to will a loss and there would be very few patients seeking an elective termination of pregnancy."

8. *I was so determined to keep my figure during the pregnancy that I kept up my usual exercise routine at the gym; then I miscarried at twelve weeks. Could I have caused the loss?*

There's little chance that you did. From what we know now, a well-established pregnancy is nearly impossible to dislodge. A pregnant friend of mine was in a car accident so severe that men with blow torches had to cut the car apart even to get her out. And still no harm was done to her unborn child. When you miscarry, it is very natural to mentally rerun the last few months to dig for whys; it is a normal part of the process of grieving. But there is no indication that strenuous exercise has any significance in pregnancy loss.

Thomas H. Green, in his medical text, says there has to be what he calls ". . . extensive local pelvic trauma . . . and even that doesn't always cause miscarriage. It is only when direct and severe accidental injury to the uterus, or to the fetus within, or to both, has occurred that trauma can be incriminated as the actual cause. . . ."[2]

9. *I miscarried once. If I do go on to have children, will they be likely candidates for deformities or handicaps?*

One study suggests just the opposite. Women who miscarried had a *lower* incidence of children with deformities. It is as if their bodies were more sensitive to problems in the growing fetuses

---

[2]Green, pp. 297–98.

and miscarried those that were abnormal, rather than carrying them to term.

10. *A woman in my neighborhood had what she called a "missed abortion." What is this?*

In a missed abortion, the baby dies but does not deliver. It is a miscarriage that only half happens. In ninety percent of the cases, labor will begin on its own a time after the baby dies, but if it doesn't, the physician will induce labor. If a woman carries a dead fetus for more that four or five weeks, she will be in some danger of hemorrhaging.

The potential for a baby to die in utero is the reason why your doctor so carefully continues to check for a heartbeat and a growing uterus. The woman may notice the situation first, if the signs of pregnancy disappear, if she shows a brownish vaginal discharge, or if the baby hasn't moved for a day or two.

Some couples prefer to wait for labor to start naturally, giving them time to prepare emotionally for the loss. But when Mary Ann and Noel's baby died at twenty weeks, they chose to have labor induced soon after the death was confirmed. "We couldn't bear waiting, knowing that our baby was dead," Mary Ann said. After about an hour of contractions, Mary Ann delivered their little boy. Her labor was short compared to that of many. It can take hours, hours that seem like days because of the sadness born from the loss.

A widely used gynecology text advises medical students about missed abortion, "Not infrequently, the extreme apprehension of the patient and her family concerning the unfortunate situation is the most difficult aspect of all for the physician to manage."[3]

After seeing the pain of Mary Ann's grief, still lingering after two years, I thought, *"Difficult, to be sure!"*

11. *I thought the testing options you discussed were only considered for "habitual aborters," women who had lost more than three pregnancies. Is this correct?*

It used to be. Studies of twenty years ago or so seemed to indicate that if you had miscarried once or twice, the probability

---

[3]Ibid., p. 302.

of another miscarriage was only slightly higher than that of a woman who had never miscarried at all. But after a third miscarriage, the studies suggested, the risk of another loss shot up to eighty or ninety percent.

But many reports in recent years have called these views into question. Researchers Warburton and Fraser, for example, found that women with three losses were *still* not much more at risk for another loss than those who had miscarried only once. Their findings looked like this:[4]

Previous Losses	% of Subsequent Losses
1	23.7%
2	36.2%
3	32.2%
4	25.9%

There are two factors that doctors now consider even *more* important than how many miscarriages you have had: Was the fetus you lost chromosomally normal or abnormal? And have you given birth to other children?

Here's why. If the fetus was chromosomally abnormal, chances are good that the loss was a random happening. But if the fetus was normal, other factors, like some of the ones discussed may have been responsible. If you have no children, a doctor might have more questions about your reproductive future than if you have had a child. Your children would offer living proof that the whole system did—and therefore probably can—work as it is supposed to.

If you want a more aggressive pursuit of answers *before* you have crossed that "magic line" of three losses (which defines you as a "habitual aborter"), most physicians will be cooperative. Particularly for women who are starting their reproductive venture later in life, waiting for three miscarriages to occur before they try to find a cause may seem like too long to wait.

12. *How do I look for a specialist, if I want one?*

There is officially no medical specialty in pregnancy loss. But some OB/GYNs have a particular interest in this problem, and

---

[4]Williamson, Table 3.

have made themselves specialists by virtue of their personal study. In the Yellow Pages of a major metropolitan phone book, for example, I found OB/GYNs who described their practice as "Limited to Normal and High Risk OB/GYN and Infertility." One family practice clinic routinely refers habitual aborters to an obstetrician with this kind of practice. This physician may, in turn, draw on the expertise of others, like geneticists, for example, if the need arises.

A reproductive endocrinologist may be able to give you the help you need, since these physicians specialize in treating infertility. Being able to conceive but not carry the pregnancy to term is considered a kind of infertility, too. University hospitals often have infertility clinics as part of their OB/GYN departments, and they may be a place where you will find special help.

An infertility support network called RESOLVE is also a good and up-to-date help in locating a doctor. By writing their national office (P.O. Box 474, Belmont, MA 02178), you can receive, for a small fee, a list of specialists in your area. In 1983, for example, RESOLVE surveyed over nine hundred doctors across the nation and classified them according to their particular specialties within the field of infertility. Though the list is not all-inclusive, it can give you a good place to begin.

You might also call your state Department of Health.[5] In Iowa, for example, the Regional Genetic Consultation Service is a joint venture of the Department of Health and the University of Iowa Hospital. It offers help to couples looking for reasons behind their miscarriage problems, and charges for its services according to the client's ability to pay. State-sponsored programs

---

[5]A word of caution. Be sure you filter medical recommendations through the grid of your own values. For example, specialists are now suggesting to infertile couples a treatment known as "ovum transfer." In this process, sperm from the husband of an infertile woman is inseminated into another woman, in hopes that conception will take place. If it does, the fertilized egg is transferred to the uterus of the infertile wife, who delivers the baby. What is the problem with this treatment? The developer of the process, Dr. John Buster, admits that "some potentially good embryos have been lost during the procedure." If you believe human life begins at conception, ovum transfer would be an unacceptable infertility treatment for you until the risk of the loss of embryonic life is eliminated. Other treatments may present similar moral difficulties, so ask questions, and weigh the implications of suggested courses of action before you move ahead.

like this vary across the country, and change from year to year with the availability of legislative funding, but a call to your state Department of Health might turn up the resource for help you've been seeking.

SECTION THREE:
RESTORING RELATIONSHIPS

CHAPTER SEVEN

If Your Doctor Let You Down

Dr. Bob Michaels pushed aside a stack of medical journals and picked up the sheet listing patient appointments for the day ahead. Mostly prenatals, he noted.

He grinned when he saw Katherine Lewell's name as his one o'clock patient. That would be a lively appointment. The twenty-year-old was one of those fresh-scrubbed, shiny blonde, cheerleader types who thought being pregnant was, like everything else in her life, "I mean, *absolutely incredible!*" Last month, she had let out a whoop they heard clear down to the appointment desk at the first sounds of her baby's heartbeat. Patients like Katherine could keep even a routine prenatal exam from being routine.

How many of these exams had he done in the last twenty-odd years of medical practice, he wondered to himself, "I should post a tally of deliveries," he thought as he tapped his pen against the desktop, "like McDonald's does about the hamburgers they've sold." And he chuckled at the image of a digital counter beside his receptionist's desk, ticking off babies delivered. Now 3,000; ten minutes later, 3,001. Delivering babies was the sort of thing he joked about, he knew, because when he tried to express how he *really* felt about being a part of those births, it always came out sounding like the poems on a cheap greeting card—sticky and sentimental and trite. How does a suburban obstetrician talk about the wonder of birth without coming off corny? The jokes about McDonald's would have to do.

A call from the hospital broke his reverie. Yes, Mrs. Wilcox could have pain medication, but nothing stronger than Tylenol 3. Let's see . . . the rest of the day. The name in the first slot was unfamiliar, Natalie Markus. Had he seen her before? No. "Three miscarriages," the notation said. "Wonders about the future."

Working with women like this Mrs. Markus had its own kinds of satisfaction for him. Helping her sort through causes and options offered a tangible way to feel like he was fighting back against this overwhelming sorrow of pregnancy loss. And he needed to feel like he could fight back. Oh, he and Margaret had had three healthy kids with no hitches, but enough times he had stood beside the hospital beds of or across the desk from women whose children had died—either by miscarriage or as stillbirths. And in the eyes of each of them he had seen the same piercing disappointment and sagging sense of failure. This Enemy was a foe worth taking on.

Mrs. Markus would make the third habitual aborter he had seen this week. As the words slipped by, he caught himself. Habitual Aborter. For physicians, a technically useful term. But for many women, a dreadful one.

He still remembered the distress on the face of one patient when he called her miscarriage a spontaneous abortion. He realized then that she had never heard the term abortion used except in the sense of terminating an unwanted pregnancy, and her baby had been anything but unwanted! No reason to defer to a medical dictionary at the expense of a patient's peace of mind. These women did, after all, have enough to deal with without having to stumble over words uncomfortable for them.

Besides the unfamiliar words, there stood, he knew, the less-easily-surmounted communication barrier of emotions. Being told your cervix may be "incompetent" isn't the same as hearing that the Los Angeles Dodgers won't make it into a pennant race this year, but unthinkingly he could treat both pieces of information as if they carried the same emotional weight. He shook his head again as he remembered one patient dissolving into tears when he mentioned the possibility of fibroid tumors in her uterus. Half a Kleenex box later, she choked out that two months before her aunt had died with a cancerous tumor on her liver.

So when he had mentioned "tumor," the word she heard was "cancer." It had taken some careful reassuring to clean up the aftermath of that unintended emotional bombshell.

His nurse tapped lightly at the door, then stuck her head in without waiting for his reply, "Ready for your first patient, Dr. Michaels?" she asked, "Natalie Markus is here." Dr. Michaels patted his pocket to be sure his stethoscope hadn't gotten lost and rose to grasp the extended hand of his new patient in a warm handshake, "Good morning, Mrs. Markus. I'm Dr. Michaels. How can I help you?"

Resolving the past.

Oh, for a Dr. Michaels in every town, in every family practice office, behind every OB/GYN shingle. Caring, competent and committed to communicate. Unfortunately, Dr. Michaels may not characterize the physicians who have treated you in the past.

It is a standing tradition in the musty Iowa farm town in which I live that after a major illness, the now-well person takes out an ad in the weekly *Reminder*, thanking those who supported him or her. It's a sort of "To whom it may concern" Hallmark card done in newsprint. And unfailingly, the list of those to be thanked includes the person's doctor. This fact strikes me as odd, since in contrast to all this good will, the women who have talked to me about their pregnancy losses rarely report any grateful feelings toward their doctors. What has surfaced instead is anger, even bitterness. I have heard four standard complaints: the doctor didn't seem to care; the doctor might have made a mistake; the doctor didn't do what was expected; the doctor made decisions that the woman wouldn't have made. Each of these complaints needs to be explored.

"My doctor didn't seem to care."

"He could have called," Margie lamented after her miscarriage. "The New York City doctor my cousin works for took time out from her vacation in the Bahamas to call her patients who'd lost babies—just to see how they were doing. Ours didn't even seem to care."

Dr. Barbara Batts, a Kansas City gynecologist and obstetrician, says she always tries to help a woman and her husband prepare for the grief they may experience after a miscarriage. "It's an inadequate treatment to only care for the physical aspects of miscarriage," she asserts. But judging from the sample of women I've talked to, Dr. Batts tends to be the exception rather than the rule. During my four miscarriages, I was treated by seven different doctors, none of whom ever indicated that I might experience mourning or that more than just my body would need healing. Because of what the doctors *didn't* say, I assumed that my depression was inappropriate.

In his medical textbook (one your doctor probably poured over in medical school), T. H. Green tells aspiring physicians that physical treatment is important, but "perhaps more important is the development of a close, supportive relationship between physician and patient, the . . . [doctor] constantly offering reassurance and encouragement at the regular prenatal visits and also remaining readily available in the intervals between."[1] In the margin beside this admonition, I scrawled, "Wouldn't this be great?"

Dr. Robert Bremner, a family practitioner, looks at himself and his colleagues and observes, "I see the role of a physician as a delicate balance between scientist and artist. As a scientist, he must be studied and objective, uncovering data, evaluating findings, making decisions about treatments. But the artist role demands that he also be a people-person, warm and caring, and skillful in *communicating* compassion. In medicine, as in most arenas of life, the perfect blend of scientist and artist is rarely seen. I believe there are many physicians who care deeply about their patients, but simply do not know how to let patients know their concern."

But perhaps in response to increased pressure from patients and society's growing concern for the emotional ramifications of of miscarriage, changes may be occurring. Indeed, at a recent

---

[1]Green, p. 304.

conference of the American College of Obstetricians and Gynecologists, its twenty-four thousand members were urged to *talk* with patients who lose a developing or newborn child. Dr. David D. Youngs, of the Maine Medical Center in Portland, observed, "Physicians have been taught to relieve pain and suffering. This pain requires the work of grieving, talking about the loss and sharing this grief."[2] Your physician's peers may be making him or her more aware of the need to lend the emotional support that could have helped you along.

"I'm not sure my doctor was competent."

"I called his office when the bleeding began, but he didn't get back to me for a whole day. By then it was all over. Perhaps if he had seen me right away. . . ." Lana's complaints are echoed in various forms by many women.

But perhaps your doctor really did do all that could be done. Remember how we talked about anger as one of the faces of grief? And that anger has to find an object? After a pregnancy loss, you may find your doctor to be the safest person in your world to get mad at. Directing anger at your husband has implications for your marriage; getting mad at God has implications for your faith. If friends become your target, you may lose valued relationships. But berating the medical profession holds none of these risks. You can rant and accuse and rail all you like, and then simply go find a new doctor for the next pregnancy, leaving your former physician in the ashes of his or her crumbling reputation.

Diane Bierke-Nelson, a genetics counselor, remarked that she often sees this anger-transferral in her work with clients. "After we consult with a couple, our director sends them a feedback sheet to evaluate how helpful the consultation was. When a couple reports they were dissatisfied, we contact them again to find out how we could have done things differently. And interestingly, more times than not, the clients can't pin down any specific complaint. We sometimes become a dumping ground for the justi-

---

[2]Carey, p. 4D.

fiable unhappiness they feel over unexplained pregnancy losses or handicapped children. They don't like the blow life has dealt them; they wanted us to change it, we couldn't. Their frustration and helplessness has been turned back on us, and there's nothing we can do to change it."

Now, there are those doctors who do make mistakes, terrible mistakes with life-or-death consequences. The doctor who delivered Elaine and Scott's first son failed to take into account Elaine's acute hypoglycemia and the effects it would have on the baby during a long and strenuous labor; their son is now brain damaged. With the proper care, John would have been normal.

If you continue to be plagued with nagging questions about the medical care you received, you have a right to copies of your medical record. Talk them over with other physicians whose competency you trust.

"My doctor didn't come through with what I expected."

For those of us pushed through the post-Sputnik, science-and-math cramming school curriculums, there festers an unspoken expectation that science conquers all. And what is a doctor but a souped-up scientist? In my case it was three years before I forgave one of my doctors for what I believed was his responsibility for the pregnancy losses. Because the doctor had probed into possible causes of my miscarriages, and had run some tests, I built up hopes Mike and I would succeed on a next try. When I lost the baby, I was furious! White-Coated Wonder had broken his promise to me, unspoken though that promise was.

Now, hours of medical interviews later, I see that his advice to try again didn't originate from any sure information about the outcome of the pregnancy. His tests only showed there was no blatant problem, so he played the odds that I'd be successful on another try, since seventy to eighty percent of habitual aborters are. The fault was probably as much mine as his. I never really understood the test—what they proved and what they didn't. So I escalated his nod of encouragement into a rock-solid expectation. I should have asked more questions, pushed harder to find out what he was testing for, and why.

Any responsible physician will encourage you to ask questions. You, after all, have the final say over what happens to your body. A doctor's role is to help *you* make the right decision for *you*, not to do the deciding for you. One woman went to her doctor's office after miscarriage, and found herself undergoing an unexpected D and C in a hospital operating room that same day. The surprise of being shipped off to the hospital so quickly proved to be almost as traumatic as the miscarriage. She later learned there was no medical reason her D and C had to be done that day. Just because her doctor said, "I'm calling the hospital to check you in . . ." didn't mean she had to mindlessly agree without asking why, and insisting on a satisfactory answer.

You may, however, find this logical advice difficult to apply. I did. For one thing, my pride wouldn't allow me to pour out, to this near-stranger behind his oak desk, how confused and frightened I felt. And I didn't understand why all the emotions surrounding these losses seemed to drop a thick, foggy cloud over my brain whenever my doctor would talk about medical options and the future. Outwardly I sat listening, legs crossed, hands folded. Inwardly I ran scared. I didn't want to be there, didn't want to have to make decisions about a hysterosalpingogram (was that really what he'd said?). I wanted to be home. I wanted to be snuggling close to my own little baby. Quietly. Simply. Just like everyone else in my world seemed able to. Talk about a communication gap! My doctor would have been amazed at how much confidence I placed in his few hopeful words—and how disappointed I was in him when the baby miscarried. Of course he never knew. I simply changed doctors.

Instead of running, I should have made my expectations and disappointment clear to him. When I didn't understand the information I received, I should have said so, and given him an opportunity to explain. If, however, you've given your physician the opportunity to explain, and he or she doesn't come through, a change might well be in order.

"My doctor didn't share my life view."

By the time Marcia reached the doctor's office, she expected to lose this pregnancy. She had the same signs prior to her last miscarriage—the spotting, the slight cramping. And after a pelvic exam, her doctor suggested she check into the hospital at once for a D and C. "Let's go ahead and get it over with," he told her firmly. So she did.

But three years later, questions about the decision nag at Marcia. "Knowing what I know now about miscarriage, the doctor might have decided what he did because he saw that my cervix was dialated. I don't know for sure, he never said. But now I wonder if the pregnancy was really doomed. I know now that he does elective abortions, so perhaps he didn't view the D and C with the same seriousness as I would have if I'd thought there was *any* chance of the pregnancy continuing. What to him might have been just an embryo was to me a tiny forming life."

If Marcia had initially sought out a doctor who shared her convictions about the beginnings of life, she could have protected herself from these doubts. But now that it's over, how can she resolve her feelings? There is a place for reviewing medical records, and expecting doctors to take responsibility for mistakes. But what about the times when no mistake can be proved, yet bitter feelings toward the doctor still fester inside?

Letting go of the past.

What's done is done. Or is it? Sometimes hurt or anger about the past can hang on, irritating the present and confusing the future. Author Evelyn Christenson has some interesting perspectives on these hurts.

"We may feel," she says, "there is a personal gain in the satisfaction we derive from exercising our 'right' to refuse to give up our angry, negative, accusing, wounded spirit. But in reality just the opposite is true. We are the *loser*. The emotional and physical *gains* come when we take our spiritual eraser and wipe the ledger clean—by forgiving."[3]

The need to forgive those who have hurt us is a theme that starts in Genesis and runs straight through the Bible to Revelation. And it is repeated so often in Scripture because forgiveness

---

[3]Christenson, pp. 125–126.

is an absolute necessity for life as God intended it to be lived. "But how can I forgive my doctor?" you wail. Maybe you still can feel the sting of humiliation or the helplessness caused by how he or she treated you.

Myrl recalls a time when she struggled with accepting God's perspective. "I was pregnant again, and so happy! But then the spotting started, and because of my losses before, I knew full well what might be ahead. But I knew by now, too, that there was nowhere to go but to God. So I got on my knees, and half to myself, half to God, asked, 'Do I really believe You can give me this baby, normal and full-term?' And everything in me responded, 'Yes, Lord, I know You can do it. You've said, "I am the Lord, the God of all mankind. Is anything too hard for Me?"[4] And Lord, NOTHING is! Nothing can stop You—not my body, not my doctor, not my age; not anything. If You choose this child is to be, it will be.' "

Myrl had set the battleground where it belonged—between herself and God. She saw beyond the circumstances and people in her life to a God more powerful than both.

But as Myrl prayed, she remembered a Scripture passage she had heard often before. It summarized years of Israel's rebellions against God: "In the wasteland they put God to the test. So He gave them what they had asked for, but sent leanness to their soul."[5] God *could* give her this baby; she had settled that. But what if God knew it was best to say no to her desire for this child's life? She believed that God loved her, and that He had committed himself to work all things in her life together for her good. Perhaps He knew that in some way that she couldn't now understand, having this child would not be for her best. The Israelites insisted that their desires work out *their* way and nothing less. So God acquiesced, but the results were not all they had hoped for. They ended instead with emptiness and unfulfillment. Would she do the same if she insisted on her own way?

"As I had before at points of crisis like this one, I yielded," Myrl said. "I told the Lord how very much I wanted the baby.

---

[4]Jer. 32:27.
[5]Ps. 106:15, King James Version.

But He knew what was really for the best. I didn't. So I gave Him freedom to do with this pregnancy whatever He chose. And He responded at once with a marvelous peace about the future, and a settling sense of His love for me."

Making peace with your doctor may begin with your making peace with God. And with that peace, you will have the needed resources to forgive and be free.

CHAPTER EIGHT

Protecting Your Marriage

Their newborn son's name was Andrew Philip, a combination of her name, Andrea, and his, Phil. That special name was to be a symbol of their combined lives and love to produce this, their first child. But after nine months and three weeks of anticipation, Andrew Philip died in utero and was delivered stillborn.

Six months have passed since his death, but as Andrea talks about him, the wounds are still open, still very fresh. "This pain doesn't go away in a month," she acknowledged with a shake of her head, "or in two . . . or in six." The grief hangs on like a parasite. Tears intrude without warning.

This sadness chose some unlikely candidates. Phil and Andrea are one of those strong, bright couples who warm themselves into your life without your even knowing it has happened. They've retained enough of their Detroit auto-worker heritage to show some fight, but they've assimilated a strong dose of the folksiness of their new Colorado home. Positive, optimistic, funny. They are people who are going places, happy in their relationship with God, in love with each other, excited about life. Or at least that's how it was.

It's not that they had never known tragedy, prior to Andrew's death. Andrea's alcoholic father died when she was just fourteen. And a few years ago, Phil nearly lost a leg in a severe motorcycle accident. Their recent move involved suffering of a sort, too. Phil wanted to try selling insurance, so the job offer in Colorado sounded appealing. Andrea went reluctantly. Detroit was her home, centering ground for her huge Catholic family. And her job at the travel agency held bright promise for the future. Besides, she was a city girl so a small-town pace turned out to be more boring than relaxing, more isolated than private. But Phil worked hard to help her like it, and she had in turn, tried hard not to grumble for his sake.

Then she became pregnant. Choosing a doctor brought on another of those city girl/small town conflicts. Andrea felt uneasy about not having an obstetrician, but the closest one practiced in Denver, a full hour away. And she had done enough complaining about the limitations of this town, she decided. She would just go to a local family doctor and say no more about it. Phil drove her to every appointment.

As her belly swelled, the child inside became more real, especially after he chose a four-hour stretch every night (11 p.m. to 3 a.m., like clockwork!) to kick and wrestle and generally make his presence known. These middle-of-the-night wakenings became Andrea's time to be with him, patting him, visualizing him. "This baby had my personality. I knew it." Andrea said. "He could let you know what he felt already, like his hatred for peanut butter. He'd be aggressive when he grew up. A go-getter." She started a diary of her feelings about the pregnancy and her growing love for this little one.

Andrea's due date passed—then one week and still another, with no sign of impending delivery. At their Thursday morning appointment, Phil approached the doctor about getting a sonogram, just to be sure everything was all right, but the doctor waved him off. "You're worrying unnecessarily," he assured Phil. "First pregnancies are often overdue."

That night, Andrea passed what she guessed was a little bloody show, and began to feel pressure in her lower abdomen. The beginnings of labor at last, they sighed. But labor didn't begin, though on each of the next three days there was a little more bleeding. On Sunday night, the 11:00 kicking session didn't come. By Monday the baby was kicking again, but not with the same force as before. All day Wednesday Andrea felt no movement, but she resisted her urge to call the doctor. "We have our regular appointment tomorrow morning," she told Phil, "and if I call today, he'll tell us just what he has every time we've brought something up—'There is nothing to worry about.' We asked him last week about the sonogram. If something was wrong, I'm sure he would have checked it out by now."

On Thursday morning Andrea woke up at 5 a.m. crying. Phil shook his head to clear away the sleep.

"Honey, what's the matter?"

"I don't know," Andrea wept, "but I feel so empty. I think something is very wrong. Will you hold me?" And Phil pulled her close while she cried. A few hours later they drove silently to the doctor's office. The doctor checked and rechecked Andrea's abdomen. "I can't find a heartbeat," he finally admitted, and Andrea felt the hope drain from her. The doctor was saying something about going to the hospital across the street for more tests, but Andrea barely heard him. Their baby was dead. Somehow she got up from the examination table and pulled on her clothes for the walk to the hospital. When Phil saw the tears streaming down her face, he picked her up in his strong arms and held her as she choked out the news.

Hard labor began almost as soon as the IV was punched into her vein, and the contractions went on for nearly eighteen hours. Their childbirth classes had prepared them for a long period of mild pains, but not for unrelenting contractions every few minutes. Word of their trauma went out, and ten friends gathered at the hospital to wait and pray for Andrea and Phil through the night of labor. Partway into the night, Andrea's right leg went numb. The pinched nerve in her leg that had bothered her occasionally before was being irritated by the contractions. But their friends prayed, and feeling and movement returned.

The night dragged into morning. Phil left the labor room for a moment to report to their friends, and as the door closed behind him, Andrea felt her last reserves drain away. "Lord, I can't take any more," she sobbed. "Please . . . please. This is so hopeless. Bring this baby now." And the baby delivered.

It was a boy, a beautiful, perfect boy with a halo of soft blonde curls circling his tiny face. He was their son, right down to the straight little squared-off toes that matched his mother's. "Some place kicker this boy would have made," Tom said softly, touching his little feet. They both held him, and kissed him, and cried.

Andrea left the hospital Saturday, the day after Andrew was born. Opening the door to their silent house, she and Phil felt the full weight of their loss come crushing down on them. The trip to the hospital wasn't supposed to end like this. Coming home was going to be a victory celebration, not a time of aching emptiness. Andrea walked slowly to the nursery, all primed to enfold the warm sweetness of a new life. As she turned and closed the door behind her, it was as if a part of their lives closed behind her, too.

Saturday night friends, and friends, and more friends arrived, all wanting to help. Everyone wanted to say something, but there was little to say. Both Andrea and Phil talked with them, determined to be strong for the sake of these who so wanted to support them. But after the last one had left, Andrea collapsed in the rocking chair, and Phil went into the baby's room alone to cry the tears he had been holding back. Then he came to Andrea, and kneeling by the rocker, put his head in her lap as they embraced and cried together. She stroked his hair as she wept to herself, "This is so unfair! This should be my baby's cries I'm comforting instead of my grieving husband's."

Sunday morning more friends came, this time to clean the house and deliver food. In the early afternoon the minister took Phil and Andrea to join their friends for the graveside service. His words were simple and kind. He told about their son's name— Andrew Philip—and how it represented his parents' shared life and love for him. Andrea didn't remember much else, except that she needed to see him one last time. And before they left the tiny coffin, she lifted the lid to kiss her son once more, this time in a final goodbye.

Phil's mother arrived from Detroit on Monday. "We spent the next week talking and crying," Andrea recalled. "She had lost a baby when he was six days old, so she knew the feelings engulfing us."

For Phil, going back to work seemed impossible, but he willed himself to do what he had to. And he held up well, except for the two episodes in the grocery store when buddies spotted him and asked, "Did your baby come? What did you have?" Both times he cried as he told them of Andrew's death. He had determined, though, to be strong for Andrea, so during the next weeks, when grief would well up, he choked back the tears and tried pretending it was over. But the strain of holding back soon took its toll in his usual open relationship with Andrea. She was the one who sensed what was happening. "You can't do this," she told him. "I can't live with not knowing what you're feeling." So they talked and cried together, both assuring the other there was no blame. They may have lost Andrew, but they determined they would not lose their life together, too.

Six months have passed since Andrew's death. But when she talks about the loss, Andrea expresses a jumble of feelings—anger and guilt and regrets and questions about the future.

"We've tried not to be mad at our doctor," she sighed, leaning back in her chair. "We've wondered about suing him, but it probably wouldn't do any good." The new obstetrician she now sees in Denver guessed there was a problem with the cord gradually cutting off Andrew's oxygen supply. "This new doctor says nothing could have been done, but we still wonder." Andrea drops her head as the weight of the words settle in.

And there is anger at the injustice of Andrew's death. For Phil, it shows itself when he sees others no more deserving than they who have healthy babies, especially two women who were pregnant at the same time as Andrea. "One has never been much more than a tramp—lots of men, lots of drugs—and she had a perfect baby," Phil said with a touch of bitterness. "Another who did drugs for years just gave birth to a beautiful child. Where is the justice in all this?"

But more subtle and more gnawing is the guilt. Andrea wonders now if she was under too much stress, fighting the move from the city. Could that have upset the pregnancy or caused her baby to have a lesser chance? Or what about the way she gave up when the doctor announced he heard no heartbeat. She agreed then that her baby was dead. Could he have lived if she hadn't given up so easily? Did he sense the fight going out of her, so he let go, too, of his life? "I still have flowering plants that people sent, and I *have* to keep them alive," Andrea said. "There's some strange connection inside about not letting them die. It's like I'm making up for my helplessness in Andrew's death."

The sadness seems to attack them at such unexpected times and places. Like the time Phil's friends started swapping those bragging-daddy stories. Or at the women's conference when all the my-baby-your-baby small talk cut Andrea to the quick. Or the afternoon Andrea spotted a lady wearing the same maternity top she had worn, and the glimpse brought hot tears. "I still can't handle those 'We lost a baby and now we have eight children' kinds of stories. I know objectively we likely will have children, but Andrew's death is still too close to draw comfort from that fact."

These are the sounds of a grief still in process. Phil and Andrea are on the road to recovery, and given time, they will sort out the right answers. In the future, there will likely be less hostility toward their doctor. And they will be better able to see the self-accusations for what they are—unfounded, untrue. Beneath the fears and complaints and regrets are two people wanting to trust God. But for now, all the questions, all the doubts must be voiced before they can hear God's words to them. They are a corporate Job, and crying out will ready them for healing.

What is especially beautiful—and perhaps unusual—about their story is the way they grieved together. Phil and Andrea's relationship emerged stronger from the crisis. "Phil and I are better friends for having gone through this," she notes. "We're connected in a way we weren't before." But they are the minority. Well over half of the couples that experience the death of a child are in some stage of separation within a year after the death.

One author explains, "Bereavement tends to make all of us very self-centered just at a time when we need to be supporting our suffering spouse. The loss of a child can hit us so hard that we wonder if we shall survive. The marriage relationship then definitely becomes a secondary factor; our own survival is primary. We become self-centered in the extreme. The glue that holds a marriage together is directly opposite to self-centeredness; it is caring about and for another. When we cease caring about the other and focus on ourselves, trouble is sure to erupt."[1]

---

[1]Tengbom, pp. 9–10.

A marriage can be deeply strengthened by a shared sorrow, but it always takes work to bring about that strengthening.

Lessons on marriage and mourning.

Your relationship can grow through the pain of your loss if you consider four suggestions: Decide that your marriage will come out stronger. Accept the fact that you and your husband will sorrow differently. Let others help. And don't place God-sized expectations on your partner.

Determine you'll come through it together.

The death of his father was the deepest tragedy of Neil's life. Neil had lost his guide, his mentor, his closest friend. After the funeral Neil accepted all kinds of new positions in the service clubs his father frequented. One office led to two . . . then three. The long hours he spent at the bank were multiplied now by evenings and weekends away at meetings. Ann and their two small children felt abandoned.

But Ann determined she would talk—and listen. One afternoon as they reminisced about his dad, Ann began to cry. "I'm sorry, Neil, I try to hold back for your sake. I don't want you to come home to a sad wife, but sometimes I miss your dad so much." And finally Neil opened up. "I miss him, too," he admitted. "But I feel like I have to carry on, for Mom's sake, you know. And all those clubs I've joined, it's like I have to fill all the places Dad did, now that he's gone."

The insight Ann and Neil both gained from their conversation drew them closer together. When they understood that Neil's new passion for volunteer work was but his way of grieving, Ann could accept his absences with more grace. And Neil could finally admit that trying to replace his dad would not bring him back.

You can allow the loss of your child to drive you and your husband apart. Or you can use the difficulties to bring you to a deeper understanding of each other. The choice is yours, but it does require a choice.

Uncover, and then accept your differences.

Even though you may be close, you and your husband will have differences, differences in what the loss has meant to you, in how you grieve, and in what you see as comforting.

The loss may hold a different meaning for each of you. Your husband may be plagued by feelings of failure. You look to him for protection and care; but in this crisis of miscarriage, he stood by helplessly while your child's life was lost. Afterward, you are terribly unhappy, but his attempts at comfort don't seem to work. He's helpless again.

Or your husband may have had fears he never expressed during your pregnancy. Worries plague many men as they look ahead to the arrival of their child. Husbands fear for their wives' health through the pregnancy and delivery. The added financial responsibilities cause concern. They wonder how their relationship with their wives will change as the baby comes. And they may worry over just how successful they will be at this whole task of fathering.[2] After the loss of your baby, your husband may be struggling with issues of which you are unaware.

And maybe you have feelings *he* can't comprehend.

This was especially true for Joleen after her second miscarriage. "Our son Brad was four by then," she recalls, "and the joy of my life. My dream had always been to be a mother. Caring for Brad produced all the satisfaction I'd thought it would. But with these miscarriages came the question of whether we'd ever be able to have more children. To me, a lady with just one child simply couldn't define herself as a first-of-all, full-time, life-time mother. One child just wasn't enough to require that level of commitment. So I felt very empty. What was I going to live for, if what I wanted to live for couldn't be? But my husband's life direction was unaffected by the losses."

Hannah and her husband Elkanah lived through just such a conflict. The Bible says this godly Jewish couple enjoyed a sweet and loving relationship. When Hannah wept over her barrenness, her husband tried his best to comfort her.

But the words of consolation he chose pointed up the distance

---
[2]Kennell and Klaus, p. 112.

that can exist between two loving people. "Hannah, why are you weeping? Why don't you eat? Why are you downhearted? Don't I mean more to you than ten sons?"[3] Though he loved his wife, Elkanah could not understand why a good husband couldn't make up for not having children.

You may express sorrow differently. Phil shed more public tears at Andrew's death than did Andrea. Her grief came out more as anger—anger at the doctor, at the healthy babies of others, at herself for what she might have done differently. But as Andrea explains, "You have to remember that my dad died when I was fourteen. And when he did, there was no time for much melancholy. I started looking for a job—I had to, for the family's survival. So when we lost Andrew, it was instinctive for me to act strong, first for the sake of those waiting with us in the hospital, then later for those at the funeral. I don't see it as the best way to mourn, but Phil understands that I'm hurting the same as he is. It's just that with my background, I simply can't let go in front of others."

You may offer comfort differently. Some couples go through deep difficulties because of the differences in what comforts them. Sometimes the bedroom becomes a battleground. The wife may say, "Our baby has been gone just a few weeks, and my husband wants to make love! Oh, I know the doctor says it's okay, but how could we? Sex . . . sex is for pleasure and for making babies. We've just failed at the making babies part, and the way I feel now, nothing will give me pleasure again for a long, long time. Doesn't he care that our baby is gone?" She may want to be close and derive great comfort from just being held, but intercourse denotes something more. Not comfort, but perhaps an act of indulgence, an indulgence inconsistent with the harsh realities with which she is having to deal.

But for her husband, making love may be a means of comfort, of being comforted. Carol remembered the pain her husband endured as he stood by helplessly through his mother's death due to cancer. After a day at the hospital with his mother, Joe came into the house late at night and up to their bedroom where

---

[3] 1 Sam. 1:8.

Carol was reading. "Do you want to talk about it?" she asked. "Not now," he shook his head. "After." And they had made love. For Joe, it was an emotional escape, a deep sharing that eased the pain. Had Carol not understood, she might have refused, leaving Joe feeling even more alone.

You need to understand the way your partner grieves, as well as help him understand what comforts you.

Let others help you.

When your husband cannot completely meet your needs, or you his, you'll be tempted to conclude that your relationship is grossly lacking. Often a downward spiral of hurt and blame and withdrawal can begin. But you have not failed, nor has your husband, if you cannot be each other's total resource during this time.

Mildred Tengbom counsels couples that it doesn't always work to tell each other everything. "Sometimes it is not even wise, especially to begin with, for spouses to try to communicate—at least too vividly or frequently—their hurt to each other. Sometimes it is wiser to find someone else to whom you can unload."[4]

During your grieving, it may be a great help to look for others outside your relationship in whom to confide. Phil and Andrea, you remember, drew upon his mother as a resource. Sometimes there is a level of emotional identification over a pregnancy loss that only another mother who has lost a child can feel. Jill found tremendous solace in writing letters to three friends who had also miscarried.

I'm not suggesting these others you talk with *replace* your husband. To grow in your love and understanding of each other, the deep feelings that surround your miscarriage will have to be shared with your mate. But there will be times during your grief when an outside perspective can help preserve and strengthen marital oneness.

---

[4]Tengbom, p. 44.

Don't expect your spouse to be Jesus Christ to you.

Unlike Phil and Andrea, my husband and I didn't grieve together after our miscarriages. Later, as Mike read some of my journal entries during the years of the losses, he was surprised at how clearly I had perceived each of them as a baby dying. Though he believes that life begins at conception, emotionally it didn't grab him as it had me.

But of course my involvement was different! Almost from the day of their conception, those babies changed my life. They demanded that I recognize their presence through the changes in my body. Clothes I was wearing got too tight as my stomach rounded. Foods I once enjoyed now made me green.

Objectively, I understood why Mike felt more removed. But disappointment still plagued me over the fact that he couldn't see the losses through my eyes. God has pushed us into one of those gut-honest, best-buddy relationships in which I breathe with this man, and he with me. A while back we were talking about people involved in extramarital affairs when I asked him, "If you were attracted to another woman, who would you go to help you deal with it?" I expected him to name a pastor, a Christian friend, or some counselor.

He thought a minute. "Gee, honey, I'd only share something like that with my best friend. I guess I'd talk to you." And we both laughed. His response was so indicative of the friendship we've hammered out in these years together. And I was prepared to name him as the one in whom I would first confide.

Because of our openness, Mike's inability to comprehend the feelings of the miscarriage, feelings which so engulfed me, hurt. But I've realized that two becoming one does not mean two becoming the same, even at points where we really want to.

Fortunately there was never a question between us about his love for me or about the completeness of my value to him, even without bearing children. And there was never any intimation on Mike's part of blame. He responded to the losses with a steady trust in God's sovereignty and a determined belief for future success.

Now, looking back, I can see that my disappointment turned

for our good. It drove me back to God and helped me keep my expectations of Mike in realistic proportion. It is very easy, especially if you have a good marriage, to sometimes slip into the error of expecting your husband to fill the place that Jesus Christ should to you. When Mike can't fill all my needs, either because of misunderstanding or because of the limitations of his own humanness, it forces me to turn, as I should have at the first, to Jesus Christ for the sense of fulfillment I desire. And with the resource of His comfort and understanding, I then have a solid basis to love and be loved by my husband.

Marriage, like any living thing, demands care and cultivation, especially after a crisis like pregnancy loss. But the investment is worth making. You lost enough when you lost your child. Make your marriage a place where both of you gain.

CHAPTER NINE

How to Help Your Friends Support You

During the emotional quagmire of my miscarriage years, my friend Loretta twice splurged to buy me nightgowns—silky, slinky, seductive gowns, too expensive to fit our limited budget and far too beautiful to be deserved by the failure I felt I'd become.

I received them reluctantly, guiltily, but my friend wasn't offended. She knew more than I did how acutely I needed these tangible reassurances of my worth and my womanliness.

But you may not have enjoyed the luxury of such sensitive support. Like many women I talked to, you may have found that some of the deepest hurts of your pregnancy loss were inflicted by those you considered friends. What happened? And what do you do now with these bruised relationships?

Some friends do not try to help.

When you lost your baby, you were forced to *deal with death*. Some of your friends have not yet considered death, nor do they want to. Staying away from the sorrowing allows them one more chance to push this whole ugly confrontation into a corner for another day.

The yellow-ballooned birth announcement said "Twins!" and Sue smiled her approval. The new parents, Wayne and Shirley, had been her casual friends from way back, but she'd lost touch with them the last few years. Apparently they'd settled in North

Dakota, or so their return address indicated, and now they'd begun a family. Good news! She would save absorbing the weight-and-length statistics for later, she decided, so she could get right to the short hand-penned note that fell out of the announcement. "We did have twins," Shirley wrote, "but Sara Beth died just two hours after birth. Todd Andrew is an unbelievable joy, but we're still very sad at our little girl's death."

Sue mulled for days over how she would respond. Would a gift for their son be inappropriate? Or should she write a note of sympathy? But if she did, what would she say? What *do* you say to a young couple whose little girl has just died? And underneath, there rumbled resentment at Wayne and Shirley for telling her about their daughter. "If only they'd just not sent me an announcement. After all, we hadn't seen each other for years, and we've lost touch with most of our mutual friends. I wouldn't have known," Sue grumbled.

She steamed and stewed about it, and finally decided to do . . . nothing. As far as Wayne and Shirley knew, Sue never received the news. But later Sue would admit, "I know now my conflicting emotions weren't generated by animosity toward our friends. I just didn't want to face death, even at the cost of leaving our friends to suffer alone. Some friend I turned out to be!"

Another reason why some of your friends will not want to help may be because *they've been burned before* when they've tried to comfort someone's hurts. Comforting the grieving is, for the most part, a thankless job because the bereaved give so little back. With their personal resources so low, mourners are not a joy to be with. And after the worst of the crisis has past, they sometimes seem to cut themselves off from those who did the most to stand with them.

Writing in *Christianity Today*, Pastor Ross Lakes told of several experiences in which he and his wife gave generously to people in need. (And "generously" included more than once emptying their savings account.) In one situation, they were able to save a man's business; in another, they helped a man make his house payments until he could return to work. But within weeks after every single case of large-scale giving, the receivers had become offended at the Lakes and the relationship had been lost. Now

Rev. Lakes cautions others who give so generously to do it anonymously, or they may lose a friend in the process.[1]

The dynamics of this withdrawal puzzle me. Perhaps once we are stronger, we look back on our period of grief, embarrassed that we revealed so much of ourselves and our weakness. Counselors say psychological nakedness terrifies many people. Or perhaps being with the people who helped us reminds us of a life period we would just as soon leave behind. Or maybe the humbling involved in having to be receivers with so little to give is too painful.

But it happens. Sometimes people who worked hard to help a mourner, wind up losing a relationship. So if friends avoid you in your grief, it may be because of other rejections long before your time.

Some friends may not want to help because they feel *you have let them down.* Relationships mean different things to different people. And particularly if you are one of those warm, strong, good-to-be-with kinds of people, some of those who relate to you do it because they like what they get from you. They're down, you perk them up. They're bored, you stimulate them. They're unsure, you give them confidence. They've come to look on you as someone to take from, someone they depend on to help them along.

Then you crash. And the sight of you in need disappoints them. They counted on you to always be strong and sure, and you've failed. You have always had answers for their problems; now you seem to have none for your own. Instead of seizing the opportunity to be a giver instead of a taker, they withdraw to wait for the time when you will have pulled yourself together again so things can be like they were before.

Your response to these friends who don't want to help? Don't write them off. They're not the enemy. They have had things to offer you in the past—and they will again in the future. It is just that in this particular life crisis, you will have to look elsewhere for support.

---

[1]Lakes, Ross A., "Five Good Reasons to Show Caution in Giving," *Christianity Today* (April 20, 1984), pp. 22–25.

Some tried to help, but went at it the wrong way.

I continually draw encouragement from the scriptural
sketches of the life of Peter. This stumbling saint intensely wanted
to do the right thing, but somehow it rarely turned out as he
hoped.

Take his response to the miracles on the Mount of Transfig-
uration, for example.

Alone with his hand-picked trio of followers, Jesus changed
before their eyes. "His face shone like the sun," the Scripture
says, "and his clothes became as white as the light."[2] Then from
nowhere, the long-since dead Moses and Elijah appeared, and
began talking with Jesus. James and John sat in awed silence.
But not Peter, "Lord," he blurted out, "it is good for us to be
here." (The Lord was not aware of this fact?) "If you wish, I will
put up three shelters—one for you, one for Moses and one for
Elijah."[3]

Shelters. Yes, unquestionably what these heavenly beings
needed were shelters to protect them from the sun and rain.
Poor Peter! How I wonder at him—and how I identify with him.
It's just the sort of silly, inappropriate thing I would have said.
Wanting so much to be helpful. Wanting so much to be a part of
such incredible goings-on. And some of your friends are Peters,
too.

"The best thing anyone said to me?" Lynette thought a minute. "It had to be, 'I hurt with you . . .' But the worst thing
anyone said was 'I know how you feel.' Unless they'd been through
a dozen miscarriages (as I had), or six, or three, or one, how
could they really know?"

Some of the friends who refuse to discuss your loss fall into
this category, too. They fear that talking about it will only cause
pain, and they genuinely do not want to hurt you. And some of
their "Don't feel so badly, you'll have another baby . . . " state-
ments are similarly motivated. Sometimes they offer unsolicited
advice like "You need to stop thinking about it . . ." or "Surely
it's time to put away the baby things, isn't it?" because they don't

---

[2]Matt. 17:2b.
[3]Matt. 17:4.

understand the depth of your feelings and are relating the best they know how.

Some, like Job's friends, come with the right message at the wrong time. "God punishes sin," his friends reminded Job. True, of course. The Bible is loaded with accounts of sinners punished by God for their disobedience. But the Bible teaches just as adamantly that not all bad things that happen to us are a punishment for sin. Job's friends took a genuine truth and used it as a club against their friend by wielding it at the wrong time.

The Bible has much to say about the good that can come from suffering.[4] You'll be able to comfort others when you have suffered yourself. Suffering builds patience and godliness and hope. Hurting refines your faith, so it will be strong and sure. A pain endured can lead to a special depth of friendship and identification with Christ. And more, much more. There are times when these truths offer a deep and abiding comfort. But there are also times when they only rub salt in your wounds.

Dispensing comfort is as much a matter of right timing as it is having the right words. And some of your friends may have had dreadful timing.

What should be your response to these who have tried, and failed? Forgive them, and appreciate the fact that they did, after all, try. They took a risk for your sake, a risk they could have avoided. And remember that after Job's grieving, the Lord restored his fortunes only *after* he forgave the friends who had so discouraged him.

Some wanted to help, but you made helping impossible.

You? Could you be the reason why some of your friends let you down?

Maybe your friends *don't know what you need*, either because you are too proud to ask for their help, you feel unworthy of their help, or you are simply too emotionally drained to put out the energy to ask. They are not mind-readers, and if you always answer their queries with "I'm doing just fine," even though you're not, they may believe you.

---

[4]See 2 Cor. 1:4; Rom. 5:3–5; 1 Pet. 1:6, 7; Phil. 3:10.

Or maybe you're *too hard to help*. Anger is one of the faces of grief, remember? And it is like an untargeted missile, looking for a place to land. Sometimes that landing pad can be an undeserving friend.

Danielle's child died a day after his birth, and during the raging war with grief that followed, Danielle complained about how mad it made her when people said they were sorry she had lost her baby. "I did not lose him!" Danielle retorted. "I know exactly where he is—in heaven!" Now really. The people extending sympathy meant nothing malicious. They were simply drawing on a commonly accepted and usually appropriate phrase for offering sympathy. But you can bet that most of them thought twice about what they said to Danielle on a next meeting—if they were brave enough to chance saying anything.

To the friends of those who have lost pregnancies, sociologists Peppers and Knapp advise, "Angry parents are difficult to deal with and relate to. No one likes to be around hostility, jealousy, resentment, and vindictiveness. Friends and relatives of grieving parents, therefore, need to recognize this stage."[5]

Perhaps we mourners need to recognize it, too, and take the initiative by apologizing for what we have said, when these friends wanted to help, but we could not let them.

How to help others help you.

You can enjoy more support from those around you if you know how to help them give to you. Here are some ways in which you can help others help you.

1. *Be selective in choosing those in whom to confide.* You don't rehearse the details of your sex life with just any acquaintance. Nor are you obligated to unload your grief on just anyone you meet. Look at the people in your life and choose a few, perhaps even just one in whom to honestly confide your deepest feelings. That one may be your husband, but because of his own grief, or other factors we've already explored, he may not be able to always give the comfort you seek. So open yourself to another

---

[5]Peppers and Knapp, p. 36.

friend or two. But don't expect yourself to be open with just anyone.

2. *Let others touch you.* There are times when a good hug is worth a thousand sympathy cards. One expert on pregnancy loss advises, "Parents will experience anguish, sadness, and crying. . . . This is a crippling time for most parents. It is a time for touching, holding, caressing, hugging—for physical contact."[6]

You may be an expressive person already, so touching and being touched will be a natural part of your established pattern of relating. As friends see you grieve, it will be comfortable for many of them to hug you or squeeze your hand. If you aren't by nature a touching person, this may be difficult for you. But even if you don't feel a great need to be touched, you may need to let your friends touch you anyway. Doing so may meet their need to feel like they have given you something, small gift though it is. And physical contact gives people a way to say they love you and sorrow with you, without coming out with all those awkward and shallow-sounding condolences they desperately don't want to use.

3. *Encourage your friends to talk about your child.* No matter how much we know about the grief process, there is an instinctive response whenever we see a friend in grief that screams "Don't remind her of her loss!"

A couple of years ago I visited friends whose oldest son is severely handicapped, and I told the boy's mother how much I appreciated their bringing their son to a reunion of our college friends. She thanked me, and then confided, "Now that Brian is in a live-in care facility, you'd be amazed at the people who know us well, yet talk as if we only have two children, instead of three. It sometimes hurts to have Brian forgotten like that."

Her honesty was such a help to me! At that point, I still believed that asking about those kinds of hurts would be about as gracious as questions about how much money they made. And her sharing gave me courage to probe further into her feelings about Brian. It was a probing I needed to do, because I wanted our relationship to be more than just a sharing of the good times.

---

[6]Ibid., p. 34.

And God used her open heart to poke at wounds from my pregnancy losses which I had never talked about and just barely identified.

After the D and C that followed one of our losses, I was hospitalized for a couple of days. Some of my visitors included four of the singles from the college and career church group that Mike and I were leading. As those young men and women stood awkwardly beside my bed, I knew the ball was in my court. They had taken the initiative to reach out to me, even though their caring had shoved them into unfamiliar and uncomfortable territory. I knew they wanted to do the right thing, but weren't sure what that right thing was.

So I began to talk. I told them about the loss, some details of how it happened, some of the fear and disappointment I felt. And I told them, too, of the comfort the Lord was giving me. The visit turned out to be a sweet one for all of us—mutual giving, mutual receiving. But it happened partly because I took a deep breath and started talking.

Of course you don't need this kind of intimacy with everyone. Especially if your child was stillborn, you will want to think through your answer to the inevitable question, "How many children do you have?" How you answer will likely depend on how much of your life you want to reveal to the questioner. One family we know whose child died at ten always responds, "We have four sons. One of them, though, is in heaven." And for them, it is a good response. To not include Noel in the count, they feel, negates the value of his life. But if you make a different choice, you are not denying the existence of your child. You may be, instead, sparing casual acquaintances the discomfort that such an admission often produces.

4. *Tell your friends the kind of help you need.* George Sanchez, a respected Christian counselor, says that when his wife has something that needs to be said, he often asks, "How do you need me to respond? Do you want my perspective on the problem, or that I just listen? How can I help?" Your close friends may know how to ask these kinds of questions, or they may not. If they don't, you can help them by supplying the answers. If on a particular day, it is difficult for you to hear about their children, tell them.

Or if their invitation to go shopping comes at just the right time to lift your perspective, tell them. They want to help, and you will be helping them succeed by clarifying your needs and feelings.

5. *Realize that you help your friends as you let them share your grief.* You may be doing others a favor by letting them grieve with you. If they have been through losses before, there is a wonderful therapy in passing on to you what they have gained. And if they haven't grieved yet, you will help prepare them for the experience. Perhaps it won't be so frightening or so bewildering to them since they will have gone through it once already with you.

6. *Look for people to whom you can give.* It may be your husband, your children, or someone else in need. But lifting your sights from your own pain to the needs of others is an incredibly potent therapy. Jesus continually emphasized that in giving, we become the receivers.

As Jan struggled to cope with the realization that she couldn't bear children of her own, she began baby-sitting for other people's children. "One of the little ones I kept was only five days old when his mother first left him. Somehow giving myself to that baby, and the other children, helped me face up to my own feelings about mothering, and work through them."

Friends worth having.

Some of the few bright memories around my losses shine in the faces of friends who gave themselves to me. Friends like Julie, who knew enough to climb right over all the barricades of excuses I'd erect and drag me out of the house when I sorely needed it. And friends like Mary, who took on the care and keeping of another pregnant lady she knew as a way to work out her disappointment over our loss. And friends like our neighbors, the Myers and the Minteers, who corporately put their arms around our little family, and lived with us through the toughest of the times.

One good friend can more than make up for the wounds inflicted by countless others and constitutes a treasure worth hanging onto.

CHAPTER TEN

Working Through Your Children's Grief

"I'm against explaining to Jamie what happened." Alex's voice was as deliberate as the repeated rotations of his spoon around his coffee cup. He finally tapped the spoon against the cup's rim and laid it on the the table. Kaye watched her husband's little ritual as she leaned against the padded back of the booth, letting the warm June sunshine that streamed in the coffeeshop window wrap itself around her.

Alex broke the silence, "You're not saying anything. Does that mean you think we should tell the boy, or we shouldn't?"

Kaye sighed, "It mostly means I don't know. You know Jamie has been as excited about this baby as we are . . . " And she caught herself, "I mean, we were," Kaye cleared her throat. She was not going to cry in this restaurant. She had already determined that. But this discussion about their son only revived the memory of that day at the Family Planning Clinic when the receptionist told her that her pregnancy test was positive. All those months of waiting were now behind her; they were going to have a second child! But she had controlled her joy for the sake of the other women in the reception area: two teen-age girls, huddled together, rehearsing to each other the "what-if's" of an unwanted pregnancy; an unmarried mother of two who had confided, "I'm afraid my third may be on the way." To them, a positive test would generate no joy.

How glad Kaye was that she had brought Jamie with her.

He'd been praying with his mom and dad for a baby. With him she could be excited. Once in the car, she squealed, "Jamie! The lady told me God is giving us the new baby we've been wanting so much!" And he hugged her and squealed, too.

Her miscarriage at sixteen weeks had been the last thing they had expected. And now, besides their own grief, there was the question of Jamie. What would they tell him? They batted alternatives and their consequences back and forth. Finally they concluded together that they would try right away for another pregnancy. If Kaye conceived quickly, they would pretend there had been no loss, and Jamie would never need to know that the baby he had heard about had died. "After all," Alex reminded his wife, "time to a three-year-old means nothing. Anything that takes longer than a week might as well be eight years away. To wait fifteen months for our baby to grow won't be much different to him than waiting eight months."

Alex had a point. It would be good to spare Jamie from this pain that weighed so heavy. Yes. That's what they'd do.

But the success of this plan was to be short-lived. Eight days later, Kaye and Jamie detoured from their errands to enjoy a meal at McDonald's. Actually, the McDonald's indulgence was a bit of a conscience-easer for Kaye. She knew she'd been short with Jamie and had withdrawn, but her sadness seemed to leave little energy to reach out to anyone else.

Between french fries, Jamie looked up, "Mom," he asked, "did our baby die?"

Kaye caught her breath. "What makes you think that, honey?" She struggled to keep her voice even.

"Jason told me when we were coming home from preschool yesterday. He said his mom told him."

"Yes, honey. Our baby died."

Jamie's brown eyes filled with tears.

"Come here, honey." And he climbed down from his seat to get up on her lap, as they hugged and cried together.

Kaye knew then it had been wrong to keep the truth from Jamie. "I don't really remember what I told him," she said a few years later. "I know I assured him that God loved our baby, and that the baby was in heaven now."

But Jamie was to come up with his own three-year-old way of dealing with the loss.

For the next few days Jamie lay around in his room, taking care of his favorite stuffed animal, Tigger. "I knew he was acting out his perception of what had happened," Kaye said, "because he was behaving exactly as I had in the two weeks or so before the miscarriage." And after one of these sessions alone, Jamie came downstairs holding Tigger in his arms. Kaye looked up from unloading the dishwasher.

"What is it, Jamie? Can I help you?"

Her little boy sighed a deep, long, grown-up sigh. "Mom, I took good care of this baby, but the baby died." And after that, the issue seemed to have somehow been settled inside him.

If you have other children, you will want to know how to help them after your miscarriage or stillbirth. The loss, after all, was theirs, too. And helping them will be easier if you keep some important perspectives in view.

Living through a death can prepare your children for life.

A miscarriage can provide a gentle, but very real way to begin learning about death. You work to prepare your children for every other aspect of life ahead. You warn them about patting strange dogs. You instruct them that the water in the bathtub should *stay* in the tub and is not to be bailed out onto the bathroom floor. You make sure they know that a dime is worth more than a nickel, even though yes, I know it's not as big around. The purpose of all the instruction, and the disciplining, the nagging, and the cajoling is to send them prepared into the big and complicated world that awaits them.

But in the midst of the preparations, sometimes we miss readying our children for the bigger crises of life, crises like death. Some child development experts estimate that eighty percent of all children worry about death. Perhaps that's because we do little to help them with life-and-death truths, so the world around us is quick to fill the void with TV fantasies and six o'clock news reports. Children can handle death if it is introduced by those they trust in a child-size portion. And a pregnancy loss can

provide the chance to lead your little ones into a deeper understanding of life and death.

Facing death means talking about it.

It is important that your children have the information they
need to face your loss. But the quantity and kind of information
you supply will vary according to their ages and maturity. Preschool children see death as a temporary and reversible state
since daily they can see their television Superfriends fall from
ten-story buildings and walk away unscathed. They tend to view
death as not much more than a lack of movement. Thus, it is
easier for them than older children to think that the person who
has died lives on, doing the same things but in different circumstances.

When my four-year-old niece's neighbor died, her mother
carefully explained that Pearl's body would be buried in the cemetery, but the real Pearl, the part of her inside that talked, was
living safe and happy with Jesus in heaven. My daughter likes to
picture our babies laughing and climbing on Jesus' lap and playing at His feet, much like the children in a picture from our Bible
storybook.

But for six-to-nine-year-olds, death becomes more of a scary
prospect. These are the children who sit spellbound during slum-
ber-party ghost stories and think of skeleton costumes for Hal-
loween. They are beginning to understand that death is final.
And they're realizing that everyone will die sometime, though
the impact of their own death does not yet seem real.

Ten-, eleven-, or twelve-year-olds have gone beyond the mysterious fascination with death to a perspective of sadness, loneliness, and perhaps fear. They know that if everyone dies, they,
too, will die someday.

Some experts feel that it is not until adolescence that a real
understanding of the pain of death can occur. The adolescent
himself is beginning to struggle with the pangs of separation
from parents, so concepts of loss and leaving begin to take on
new significance. Fears of one's own death are common in the
upheaval of the teen years.

Being aware of your children's changing comprehension of death will prepare you to supply additional information as the need arises. Exposing your children to death is much like teaching them about sex. The completeness of the answer you give to those "but how does the baby get in there?" questions increases as the need-to-know grows. And so with death. If your pregnancy loss happened when your other children were young, you can expect in the years ahead that talking about your baby's death will come up again and again, each time with a different emphasis and perhaps new questions.

Or you may find yourself explaining the same information more than once. I'm sure my daughter and I have gone over the situations surrounding my mother's death by cancer a dozen times. Each time we have repeated the facts. Each time we have talked about her life in heaven now. Each time we have discussed our own deaths—what it might be like for Holly in heaven; what it might be like for her here if Daddy or I died. New and mysterious concepts have been slowly sinking in. And even if they did sink in, I expect to talk about the topic again as her capacity to understand death grows.

But what do I say?

If your children are young, you will need to explain that the baby has died and why. But when you do, be careful to reassure them that "the baby was born before he was big enough to be able to live in the outside world. He wasn't a big, strong child like you." A bit of protection will ease thoughts that "the baby died, maybe I will, too." Psychologists caution against telling children that the baby "went to sleep" or "went away." Either may cause a perceptive child to reason, "The baby went to sleep and didn't wake up. Maybe I won't wake up either." Or "I wonder if Mommy will come back the next time she goes away."

When we talk about death, I often try to assure my daughter that most people live to be very old and probably the rest of our family members will. And I purposely interject into appropriate conversations that if Daddy and I were to die, Aunt Margie and Uncle Harris would take care of her until she joined us in heaven.

This is the time, too, to assure your children that the baby's death was not their fault. If your children are older, they may have resented the idea of a new baby invading their territory. And they may need a clear reassurance that vascillating feelings about a new baby are very normal, and that they in no way affected the outcome of the pregnancy.

Although this may seem an unlikely connection for a child to make, one woman in her fifties firmly believes that *her* negative feelings about her pregnancy caused her baby's stillbirth. She already had two children, and her third pregnancy hit when she was exhausted and under great stress. In a pressured moment, she blurted out, "I just wish the baby would die." Then he did. Instead of confessing her wrong thought to God and experiencing the cleansing of His forgiveness and reassurance, she has carried this weight of guilt for twenty-five years.

Some children, like Denise, talk, talk, talk about what they feel. "This makes me nervous to have everybody so sad," she says. But most children won't be so expressive. Somehow kids have an innate sense for the topics that cause friction and avoid them. On one of my grumpier days, I overheard my daughter advising her cousin, "When Mom's mad like this, you're smart not to say much 'til she cools off a little." And because your children know the pregnancy loss made you unhappy, they may be reluctant to say the things that come to mind.

Therefore it will help if you look for ways to initiate these conversations. Not every day, of course. And not in a structured "now we're going to talk about the baby . . ." session. But the everyday rhythm of life together affords dozens of opportunities to ask those "honey, do you ever wonder about . . ." questions that will let your children know that sadness is okay to talk about, and to feel, and that death is another part of life.

Let your children help you.

It is not bad for your children to see sorrow. Kids need to know that the aseptic and over-in-two-minutes mournings they see on TV are not reality. But what can harm your children is *uncontrolled* grief and *unexplained* crying for which they feel they might be responsible. If you're crying, tell them why. "Mom's not mad at you, honey. It's just that seeing Nancy's baby this morning made me think of our little baby, and that I miss her. I know she's safe with Jesus, and the time will come when I won't miss her quite so much. But for right now, it's hard to have her be away from us."

Children seem to have a sixth sense about any disruption in the emotional tenor of their home. When you're under pressure, they feel it. That is why it is important to keep communicating, so they know this time of sadness was not caused by them, and that it will be over.

You might give them some way to help—like sitting on your lap for a while or agreeing to play quietly while you rest a bit. You know the terrible feeling of helplessness that comes when someone you care about is hurting and there is absolutely nothing you can do; being able to help can be wonderfully therapeutic. When a close friend of ours went through some personal problems, he came to spend a few days with us. "I doubt if the time here did much for you," I told him afterward. "I'm sure you're leaving with lots of useless advice from well-meaning but ignorant friends. But it was a great help for us. To simply be able to fix your breakfast, or listen to you, or take you to lunch made us feel like we were at least doing *something*." The release from total helplessness is a sweet release, indeed.

Don't stop disciplining.

In the same way that you cry at sorrow, young children express distress by misbehaving. You may find your children responding to your grief with disobedient behavior and at a time when you're least prepared to cope with it. One temptation at these points is to simply ignore the disobedience.

Adonijah, the son of King David, grew up to be a spoiled and willful adult who tried to wrest the kingdom from his aging father. But the Bible notes about his behavior, "His father had never interfered with him by asking, 'Why do you behave as you do?'" Why was David so lax with Adonijah? Perhaps part of the answer is given in the rest of the verse: "He . . . was born next after Absalom."[1]

Absalom was David's treasured son, and even though he rebelled and caused his father indescribable grief, Absalom's death marked one of the lowest points of David's life. Perhaps in the whirlpool of sorrow that followed Absalom's death, disciplining his handsome younger brother seemed too much to ask. Perhaps David felt guilt over Absalom's death and tried to do penance for the guilt by giving in to Adonijah. Or perhaps David simply didn't have the emotional energy to care. If he responded in these ways, he was certainly not the last parent to do so. It is important for your living children that you discipline their behavior. How else will they know you still care?

But equally important is for you to realize that insecurity is often the root cause of misbehavior. Grief can also cause other signs of distress besides misbehaving. Are your children having trouble sleeping? Are they more or less talkative than usual? Do they spend more or less time alone? Your children may be telling you that they need more time with you, more assurance from you that all is still well. Like anyone in grief, children need more hugging, touching, and holding, the physical reassurances of your presence and your love.

Beware of the "sainthood syndrome."

When a baby dies, that little one leaves behind a perfect life. You never had to rouse from a deep sleep to tend to his diaper. He never spilled his milk on your mauve velvet sofa. Of course had he lived, these things inevitably would have happened. There would have been those moments when he would have infuriated you, as all our kids do. But these realities are easily forgotten in the emotional immensity of his death. And when you talk of him, it is with respect and reverence and love.

To your other children, this might lead to an incorrect answer to that inevitable question, "Who does Mom love more?" It may seem to them that the child you lost will always be more dear. If

---

[1] Kings 1:6.

you think this is unlikely, remember back to the times you've heard your well children complain as you tended a sick one, "I wish I could get sick so I'd get some of the attention around here."

Complaints about feeling unloved are normal even in the most secure of children. But you can be sure the complaints remain unfounded by being aggressive in praising your children. And communicate how much you value them, how glad you are they are in your family, how sad you would be if they were gone.

Prepare your children to talk to others about the loss.

It may help an older child to talk about what to say to other children about your loss. Depending on your children's ages, you may want to let teachers or other significant adults know what has happened so they can be ready to help.

One of the biggest excitements of our lives during the past few years was the night our farmhouse nearly became a delivery room. My sister was expecting her second child and we had carefully planned beforehand that when the baby was coming, she and her husband would stop on their way to the hospital to leave their older daughter with us. And at 2:30 one rainy, muddy morning, the call came. But when their blue Chevrolet pulled up in front of our house, Margie waddled out, white and shaky. "We're having the baby," she panted, "but I think we're having it *here*." We helped her in and onto the sofa. And sure enough, the baby was coming. But instead of a head, little toes were pushing their way out. As you can imagine, the next thirty minutes will go down in family history amid a confusion of calls to the doctor and to the emergency ambulance. By the grace of God, Jana Elaine slid safely out into a nurse's waiting hands just a few minutes later in the speeding ambulance.

During all this excitement, my sister's daughter and ours, ages three and four, buzzed around the periphery. And for the next few days, the girls acted out scene after scene of "having a baby." I decided that it might be wise to alert Holly's preschool teacher to what had happened . . . just in case. It was fortunate I did. "Show and Tell" that Friday had never before—or since—

heard the likes of what Holly related. Since sex education isn't a normal part of the Montgomery Street Preschool curriculum, at least her teacher was prepared.

If you have been open with your children about your baby's death, there is a good chance that they will not think it strange to be open with others. A bit of instruction from you ahead of time may prepare them for the reactions they may receive. And if the adults in your children's lives know how you want the loss handled, they will probably be glad to cooperate.

If there was a funeral . . .

If your baby was stillborn, there comes the inevitable questions: Should your children see the baby? Should they attend the funeral? The answers depend on their ages and of level of maturity. Many authorities feel it does much good for children to be included. Just as your baby's death needs to become a reality for you before healing can occur, the same thing can happen for your children. Again, the unknown is usually worse than the very worst known. But like any new experience, you will want to prepare your children ahead of time for what to expect. If they attend the funeral, you may want to have another adult besides yourself with them, someone who knows your children and will be able to explain the goings-on in a way that you will be comfortable with, since you will be involved with your own grief and with others who will want to comfort you.

However, there is a great likelihood that the stillbirth is behind you, and you've already made the funeral decision. Whatever route you chose, you might look later for opportunities to take your children to a funeral, and in the context of that experience, talk about your baby's death. This can become the time to probe for misconceptions and open the way for feelings to be expressed.

If you need help with your children . . .

When psychologists make observations like, "Grieving parents may find it difficult to make even simple decisions. . . ," I wonder if they understand the implications for a mother who has another child. Caring for children is little else *but* making decisions. Can she have a cookie, or can't she have a cookie? Should I let him watch just a half-hour more of TV so I can nap, even though I said no to that show yesterday?

There may be times when you feel that the care of your children is simply more than what you can manage, especially if you are at home all day with a preschooler or two. The physical and emotional demands they make tend to stretch the strongest of women. And the work of grief is just that, work. It is as if you have taken on a new and demanding job, and that job is pulling out of you some of the resource that used to be available to your children. The lethargy, the depression, the difficulty in coping with daily life take their own toll, and for the sake of your little ones, you may need some help temporarily with child-care. I found that my friends were eager to keep my child while I rested and regrouped; it offered them a tangible way to help.

But you need to be cautious about sending your children away for an *extended* period, especially if this hasn't happened in the past. A surprise and lengthy separation from you may generate much more anxiety for your child than the baby's death ever did. Researchers Trause and Irvin observe, "Sometimes during a crisis the first impulse of parents is to try to protect their children from the sadness and confusion by sending them away to stay with relatives or friends. Experience has shown, however, that . . . children manage better when they remain part of the household and experience the family's reality along with their parents."[2] Children are better able to cope with grief than they are with the emotional withdrawal of their parents.

Giving may be your way to receive.

I expect sometimes that helping our children through sorrow is as much for our good as it is for theirs.

One expert counsels grieving adults, "The parents' need for activity and restoration of self-esteem is best channeled into the

---

[2]Kennell and Klaus, p. 120.

task of supporting each other and especially into assisting their children in mastering the stress. Hard though it may be to help youngsters to understand the tragedy and to meet their needs, ultimately a parent's self-esteem is augmented most by being an effective parent. He could never forgive himself if, in his concern over one lost child, he were to lose the continuity of his relationship with the other children. Even very young children prove to be caring companions in grief, if given the chance. In working it through with his child, the parent often gains mastery himself. It would seem wise . . . if there are children at home, actively to direct the mourning parents to this task for the children's sake but also their own. *Clinically, one of the best indications of the parents' healthy progress in mourning is their ability to discuss and feel the loss with their children.*"[3]

Mandy's miscarriage at six weeks devastated her. But she found that her two little girls, though only preschoolers, comforted her in ways no one else could have. "During the week I spotted, I remember coming home from the doctor's office, and my two-year-old running up to me asking, 'You OK, Mommy? Dr. Rick fix your bottom?' She had no idea what was going on, but my welfare was the first thing on her mind. You can't imagine how much that meant. And when I'd cry, my four-year-old would hug and pat me like a mother would her child. 'It'll be all right, Mom,' she'd console me, 'You've always got me.' I so needed to know that someone else cared about my pain, but I was reluctant to tell friends what was happening because I couldn't be sure of the outcome. So the care my children offered met a unique need.

"And it helped *me* to talk to them about the loss. I dreaded telling my older daughter that we weren't having the baby after all. But I found that as I assured her of God's love and control in our baby's life, I assured myself at the same time. I'm the one who received most from the help I was trying to give."

You may find, as Mandy did, that helping your children in their grief will help toward a healing of your own.

---

[3]E. Furnam, as quoted by Kennell and Klaus, p. 286.

SECTION FOUR:
EXPLORING ALTERNATIVES

CHAPTER ELEVEN

Another Pregnancy?

After you miscarried, your doctor may have automatically scheduled you for a six-week checkup. If everything had healed well, he or she probably told you it was all right to try for another baby whenever you wanted to. But should you? I found there to be much more involved in that decision than simply the presence of a tightly closed cervix and a back-to-normal womb.

After one of my pregnancy losses I felt great pressure to become pregnant again as soon as possible. It was a grasping attempt to cover over the failure behind me with the excitement of new expectancy. But after another of the losses, I felt just the opposite. The prospect of facing another disappointment bore down upon me so heavily that I thought I could not endure. A week after the miscarriage, I splurged on two spiffy summer shorts outfits, and went from ash brown to strawberry blonde hair. It was as if I was burning bridges, cutting ties to that Pregnant Lady I had been before. And if the bridges were burned completely enough, I reasoned, there would be no way to slip back into that sorry tunnel with nothing but disappointment at the other end.

Both reactions were extremely subjective, highly emotional. And neither lasted. A decision with as much impact on the rest of your life as the one about children cannot rest on a "what I feel today" whim. So what are the considerations for a future try?

Is your body ready?

Your doctor may have confirmed that your womb is ready. How about the rest of you?

If your loss came early in the pregnancy, you may not have felt many physical side-effects. I spent the week after a first trimester miscarriage packing boxes for a major move to the farmhouse we now call home. Not only did I feel up to it, emptying that house became physical therapy. Unlike the pregnancy, it was a task I could muscle to the desired end. I wanted the rooms to empty, and they did. It afforded a sense of control in the wake of a failure over that which I had absolutely no control.

But not every experience matches that one. If you feel washed out and lazy for weeks after your loss, go easy on yourself. Your entire body has been in a huge state of upheaval—first pregnant, then not. Your lethargy may be a signal from your body that it needs recovery time. This readjustment period is a consideration as you look ahead at another pregnancy, too.

Diane Bierke-Nelson points out that her office encourages women to wait three months before trying to conceive again. "Hormone levels exert so much influence on pregnancy. We feel it simply can't hurt to give your body that extra time to get hormonally back to normal," she explains. Though there's nothing magical in that period of time, it does give your body an opportunity for one or two menstrual cycles. That means a chance to re-regulate hormones before they're off again in another frenzy of change. Of course if you became pregnant right away, you needn't sit in dread of a sure pregnancy loss. Doctors vary on this wait-three-months perspective. But since we know so little about factors influencing pregnancy loss, a short wait might be the wisest course.

Now is the time, too, to pursue any lingering questions with your doctor. If you are not satisfied with the information you get, seek a second opinion. Even if that doctor agrees with the first, the added reassurance of a second opinion can give you confidence. And there always stands the possibility that another doctor will pick up a detail the first missed. If you are not sure why your doctor has made certain recommendations, ask for an explanation. Your doctor may be operating from incorrect assumptions about your wishes or your priorities.

Are you emotionally ready?

There is nothing wrong with becoming pregnant again right away, but it is wrong if you are only seeking a stand-in for the child you lost. It is unfair to your child-to-be to expect that he or she be a replacement. Each child must be loved and accepted for himself or herself.

After their baby's stillbirth, Ray and Allison wondered if they had done the right thing about naming her. The name on her birth certificate had been in Allison's family for three generations. "What if our next is a girl? We could have used the name for her, and she'd have had it all her life," Allison asked. But their pastor assured them that they had made no mistake. "You intended that name for your first-born girl; and no matter how many children, you're still to have, none of them will—or should— replace her. You'll be glad you didn't deny her existence."

You may feel you simply can't wait to try again, either because of your age or some other life circumstance. Consequently, you may become pregnant before the pain of your loss is resolved. But let this new pregnancy be just what it is—a new pregnancy, and not a re-try of the last one, with hopes this time for a happier ending. Your child deserves as much.

Unfortunately, some couples hurry to try for another pregnancy in order to escape the pain of their loss.

We twentieth-century Americans cower terrified before pain. We get tranquilized, sedated, and distracted to hide from it. And we're so quick to try to remedy any disappointment that comes along ("Don't cry over your broken truck, darling. Mommy will get you a new one."). When there appears one who does not live by this avoid-hurt-at-any-cost philosophy, we find that person scarcely believable. Mother Teresa is such a one. In his portrait *Something Beautiful for God,* Malcolm Muggeridge says of her, "Suffering and death, to her, are not the breakdown of a machine, but part of the everlasting drama of our relationship with our Creator. Far from being an unjustifiable violation, an outrage, they exemplify and enhance our human condition. If ever it were to be possible . . . to eliminate suffering, and ultimately death, from our mortal lives, they would not thereby be enhanced, but rather demeaned, to the point that they would become too insignificant, too banal, to be worth living at all."[1]

You will survive the mourning and will be better for having experienced it. So don't try for another baby as a way to avoid this necessary confrontation with pain.

Remember, too, that a quick pregnancy is no way to shore up a shaky marriage.

Lynette had already miscarried more times than she could count ("Was it seven? Or eight? I'm just not sure."), and in desperation had chosen a tubal ligation to end the possibility of more disappointments. A few years later, when life looked brighter and her wounds less raw, Lynette made an appointment with the only surgeon in her area who attempted undoing this sterilization surgery.

During their interview, the doctor listened to her story, and then leaned over his desk toward her. "Lynette, are you doing this to save your marriage?" She assured him she wasn't. "But, Lynette, are you doing this to try to save your marriage?" No, no, she wasn't. She and Mel had been through some deep waters during those years of losses, but now their life together stood up strong and sure. The doctor studied her silently a moment. "Well, good. But, Lynette, are you doing this to try to save your marriage?"

And when Mel met with him the next week, the doctor's first question to him was, "Are you doing this to try to save your marriage?"

Why his skepticism? Perhaps it was because he had more often than not seen couples try this tactic. They had realized that their lives were pulling in different directions, and one or the other of them hoped that the shared experience of a baby might refocus them on one another.

Maybe a wife lives with the guilt of "not having given him a

---

[1]Malcolm Muggeridge, *Something Beautiful for God* (New York: Image Books, 1977), p. 101.

baby." Or the husband wonders if she is really a "complete woman" without children. Perhaps he questions his own masculine image. One woman told me her husband was amazed at the thinly disguised insinuations about his manliness (or lack of it) that came from his friends when they spoke of his childlessness.

Whatever the case, marriage has to stand on its own merits. Children *do* often enhance a couple's life together, but the solidity of a marriage can not depend on them. If it does, the foundation has already eroded and will likely give way in the future.

So what is the right reason to try again? It is the desire to share your life and your love with another. If you want a child for what you can give to him or her you are probably emotionally ready for another try.

Are you spiritually ready to try again?

Maybe you haven't yet considered the need to ask God about His desires for your future. I'm not sure Mike and I did with each of our pregnancies. Oh, I think we prayed in general about having children. And I know for certain that after our first miscarriage, we prayed with fervor that each of the following attempts would go to term. But that's not the kind of seeking I'm talking about.

The praying we didn't pursue intently enough would have come before each pregnancy attempt, asking God whether or not He even wanted us to try. I wanted children; so did Mike, so we set about procreating. Our prayers were more *when-* than *should*-oriented. And on the whole, our attitude wasn't wrong. We believed God had placed these desires for a family within us, and they certainly were consistent with His command in Genesis to multiply and fill the earth.

But there were times in the emotional upheaval surrounding the losses that my openness toward God became a fist-clenching, jaw-setting determination that "I *am* going to succeed at this business of having children." God was not giving us babies. But instead of fighting out the issue in a face-to-face confrontation with Him, I became more resolved than ever that we would get our kids anyway. It wasn't until my obstinacy had run out that I honestly sought God for specific direction about another try and waited in willingness for His answer, committed to accept whatever that answer might be.

It was six months after my episode of going blonde that I sensed the Lord beginning to speak to me about His desire regarding another pregnancy. A Christmas houseguest casually asked if we had thought about trying for another child. I don't know what I told her, but her question reopened a subject I thought I had drowned in a bottle of Miss Clairol and left behind. I'm sure others had asked the same question before, but somehow her query nagged at me in the days ahead, pushing itself into my consciousness at unexpected times. I wondered if God had chosen to use her voice as His. So Mike and I asked Him for direction, and as we did, a deep peace grew in both of us that we should try—just once more. And we did. I had no assurance what the outcome would be, but there was a sense of calm in that attempt because God had begun it. We felt confident that He would be responsible for the consequences, whatever they might be. And I knew that I would survive the outcome—emotionally, spiritually, physically.

So the question is a simple one. Have you asked God for His direction about trying again? And have you waited for His answer?

"The chances are good . . ."

If you're ready to try again, it is reassuring to know that statistics, at least, are on your side for success. Seventy to eighty percent of the women who have had even as many as three pregnancy losses *do* go on to bear healthy children. That is nearly a four-out-of-five success rate. There are many, many of us who have miscarried, even more than once, who now cluck over a happy brood of our own.

And there is little chance you need a caution about working on your general health in preparation for this upcoming pregnancy. Most of the women I know who have been through a pregnancy loss are more than a little ambitious to cover all the bases. Karla took prenatal-strength vitamins for a full year before she attempted another pregnancy. "I want to be absolutely sure my body isn't lacking any nutrients," she explained. Phyllis exercised. Rachel resigned her committee chairmanship at the Country Club as soon as her pregnancy was confirmed. "I'm cutting out everything optional so I can get lots of rest," she confided. "I want to be sure this baby has every chance." Though the outcome of each of these pregnancies most likely was not influenced by such copious attention to diet and exercise, these regimens certainly did no harm. And when they help a mom-to-be's general health, they often can lift her spirits. For each of these women, there existed the inner freedom that they had done all they knew to do. That in itself can give confidence and a release from some of the pressures of another pregnancy try.

During the next pregnancy.

All through Christine's third pregnancy, she felt comfortable and free. Oh, her last one had ended in miscarriage at ten weeks, but her energetic bundle, known to the world as four-year-old Gabriel, provided tangible proof that she could, indeed, bear children. Her doctor assured her that her loss was very likely a chance occurrence, and Christine relaxed in his confidence. Nine months of waiting and ripening produced Alice, the beautiful, perfect baby girl she and her husband wanted so much.

Your pregnant-lady days may feel just like Christine's. Some women have the enviable capacity to leave the past in the past and look to the future expectantly (no pun intended!).

I was not so lucky. As my age and number of pregnancy losses increased, so did the fears that gripped me. Like many women, I found myself holding back from anticipation of the baby growing inside, playing a little don't-get-involved-and-you-won't-get-hurt game in case we didn't make it to term again. Ah, the tolerance of those nurses at my monthly appointments! Each time they'd cheerily inquire how the pregnancy was going or ask one of those "won't it be fun to have a new baby?" kinds of questions. And each month, I'd make a point of dousing all this cheer with a sarcastic reply about how I'd already gotten this far with other pregnancies that had failed, and no, I wasn't sure at all that there would even be a baby to enjoy at the end of this odyssey of fattening up, maternity clothes, and LaMaze meetings. I'm sure they started groaning to themselves when they saw my name on the appointment schedule for the day.

And I purposely left the baby things in storage and the nursery dismantled almost until the very end, not wanting to chance a disappointment. If thinking positively has any effect on the outcome of a pregnancy, as some insist, it is miraculous I have any children at all!

But I did learn some tactics during that time that I still call up today when I need to live by faith instead of by fear.

First, fighting fear is nothing less than a spiritual battle. All my paltry self-protective devices did not protect me from fears about the pregnancy outcome. Those insidious "what-if's" edged in anyway. Thinking negatively did not make fears go away; it only drove away my joy. Fear was—and is—a satanic instrument to control our lives.

To those who belong to Christ, the Bible assures, "You did not receive a spirit that makes you a slave again to fear."[2] So when we are controlled by fear, it is not the Spirit of God doing the controlling, but rather our enemy, the devil. And all the helpful psychological counsel in the world cannot prevail in the face of a spiritual struggle. We need to draw on the power of God and ask for His help in the face of fear.

Second, Jesus Christ's sufficiency needs to become our focus. It helped me to name the worst things that might be ahead for me in this pregnancy. And after I did that, I matched each with either a time in the past that God had helped me with the particular problem or a promise from His Word that He would help.

Third, take one day at a time. There were days when looking to the end of the pregnancy and trying to visualize whether or not I could go on if it failed was just too much. And on those days, no alternatives existed but to ask Christ for His strength for that day, and then to assume He would provide it for tomorrow, too—when tomorrow came. When David walked through the valley of the shadow of death (an apt description for what some of us

---

[2]Rom. 8:15.

feel in the face of a pregnancy loss), he said, "I will fear no evil, for You are with me."[3] What David expected of God was not some neatly prepackaged outcome to each of his prayers but, more importantly, the sufficiency of God's presence. He knew that if God was with Him, the Lord would provide just what he needed for each of the steps ahead.

Please understand that I am not discounting the possibility of praying for, and then *expecting*, a baby from your pregnancy. Interestingly, in each of the two attempts at giving birth that actually resulted in our terrific kids, the Lord gave me a special assurance during the pregnancy to counter my fear. When carrying our firstborn, I was plagued with apprehensions that the baby would be deformed or handicapped in some way. I never mentioned my dread to anyone because I was too proud to want to sound like a hysterical mother-to-be. But the privacy of the fears didn't lessen their intensity.

And then, at about five months, the Lord gave a word. My husband was being ordained into the office of church deacon, and as a closing to the ordination, each of the new deacons was joined by his wife, and the congregation came by to greet each of us. When one of our church leaders, whom I greatly respected, took my hand, he said, "The Lord has given me a blessing to pass on to you. This child of yours will be safe and healthy, and all will go well." He caught my attention because in our church, mystical "direct messages from God" like this were simply not the order of the day. God used this man's reassurance to replace my anxiety with hope.

In our second pregnancy that "worked," God's peace came through my Bible reading in the book of Isaiah. He said, "Do I bring to the moment of birth and not give delivery?"[4] When I first read the verse, I thought cynically, "Of course there are times when You don't deliver! I've been through several." But in the weeks ahead, the verse came back to my mind again and again. And the assuring thought that came with it was, "Yes, Maureen, you have had disappointments in the past. But this

---

[3]Ps. 23:4.
[4]Isa. 66:9.

time is going to be different." And I slowly began to rest in this confidence.

I am sometimes reluctant to share these experiences because of the natural tendency in all of us to want to wring a promise for success out of God. And I've sometimes conveniently "found" a promise for this or that which came from my own desires rather than from God's voice. But in both of these cases I wasn't seeking foreknowledge about the pregnancy. I wasn't insisting God tell me how the story would end. In His kindness, He simply chose to do so. And in those pregnancies, He used special assurances to combat my fears.

But there were other times when there were no "words" beyond "Fear not, I am with you." His control and sufficiency were just as real. And the outcome was just as solidly in His hands. To me, the significance of these messages is that God meets us—not always in the same ways—but always at our point of deepest need.

The issue of trying again will be simpler if you look to Him first, and then trust His guidance through whatever comes.

CHAPTER TWELVE

The Adoption Option

The decision about birth control seemed easy enough. And it was a decision that needed to be made. Ted had three years left before he graduated from the university; Janeal would need to stick with her job at the printing company until he could support them. The circumstances were unfavorable for having children, and so Janeal saw a doctor for her first prescription of birth control pills.

Three years later, as Ted reported for his first teaching job, Janeal breathed a sigh of relief that her days on the Pill were over. They hadn't been her best years. She had gained twenty-five pounds and entertained frequent nausea and stronger-than-usual menstrual cramping. Of course her new doctor had said her miseries resulted from taking a dosage far too strong for her, but it mattered little now. Those Pill-popping days were over and a simple, bright future ahead. She would leave these body woes behind, conceive, and live happily ever after with her dear husband, and a sweet baby . . . or two . . . or three.

Her first menstrual period after going off the Pill might have been a miscarriage. The doctor wasn't sure. But he did feel that her unusual amount of bleeding warranted a D and C. The "*might* have been pregnant" diagnosis sounded hazy enough to Janeal to discount it. She wrote the experience off as just a bumpy attempt to start her reproductive life, and went home to try in earnest.

Several months later the test confirmed, "pregnant." No maybe's this time. And Janeal anticipated a rosy nine months of "blossoming." Wasn't that what they said pregnant women always did? Or did they "glow"? Either way, it sounded romantic and quite nice. And it would be wonderful, she knew, when this disgusting nausea and life-draining exhaustion ceased. Morning sickness was one thing. But all-day-long sickness? Everyday sickness? Regular vomiting and irregular cramping? Janeal kept at her job, but barely. Surely this misery would pass.

And it did pass, though not as she expected. When the cramping became more severe and she began spotting, a very scared Janeal called her doctor. After an exam, he cleared his throat and looked up at the ceiling and then at the floor. "Looks like you're going to lose this one. Of course, it's no surprise. We find that fifty percent of our girls who have been on the Pill miscarry their first pregnancy. So . . . go home and lie down. Don't do anything strenuous and call me when you start miscarrying. You'll know when it happens."

What? Janeal checked herself to be sure she had heard correctly. Maybe she would lose this baby because she had been on the Pill? Disbelief, then anger flooded over her. Why hadn't her doctors told her *before* about the implications of her birth-control choice?

But the anger dissolved to fear, then the fear gave way to determination. "Maybe some women lose their babies, but fifty percent don't! And *that's* the group I'm joining!" She reminded herself that unusual illnesses never happened to her. And she headed home, determined to rest and equally determined to succeed. Janeal climbed into bed, and stayed there. But by the next morning, her body ached from doubling up against the cramping. "Maybe some stretching," she thought. "I just need to unkink." And she flipped on a TV exercise show. Ah. Pulling her body hurt just enough to make her think it would relax her strained muscles. But two stretches more . . . and she began hemorrhaging.

Janeal panicked at the blood and grabbed the phone to call Ted. The school secretary must have recognized the signs of terror in her voice, because she kept her on the line while Ted was being paged, just to be sure Janeal didn't pass out. Over half an hour to the hospital. Would there be a chance to save her baby? Janeal desperately hoped so. But she was barely on the examination table before she realized that the medical staff didn't consider saving the baby a possibility. And her heart sank with the realization of what was really happening. Ted took her hand the moment before she was wheeled down the hall toward surgery, and told her he was going back to school to tie up some loose ends, but he'd be back. In a moment, the anesthetized haze became darkness.

Through her groggy post-operative fog, Janeal could see Ted leaning over her, a dozen roses in one hand, a new outfit for her in the other. But she could not return his weak smile. The new emptiness in her body had already been refilled with immense guilt and bitter anger. The doctor had told her to rest. Why had she done those exercises? Had she taken her baby's life with her stupid stubbornness? And what about Ted? Couldn't this man of hers take two hours away from those precious high-school students of his to *stay* with his wife through the worst crisis she had ever faced?

The aftermath of the miscarriage brought out all sorts of negative emotions Janeal had never seen in herself. Just before she left the hospital, she had walked down to the nursery to see the newborn babies. But as she stood at the nursery window, the realization of her loss suddenly felt like an eight-ton boulder bearing down upon her. She felt herself beginning to faint. A nurse realized what was happening and helped her back to her room.

But avoiding the nursery couldn't keep her from avoiding pain. There was the hurt when a lady consoled, "It's Nature's way of getting rid of deformed babies before they are born." Another told her it was God's way of solving the same problem. "I've got a better plan for both Nature *and* God," Janeal thought caustically. "Just don't allow deformities. Or don't let people get pregnant. Or give me a baby with a deformity. I could live with it if the baby was *mine*."

But most of her anger found a target in Ted's work. And a marriage that had been up to now more than just congenial became one on-going fight. "Ted, I didn't get married to live alone," she would complain. "Monday and Tuesday and Wednesday nights are football practice. Thursday night is the Junior Varsity game. Friday night you coach the Varsity team. Saturday morning you watch game films; Saturday afternoon it's college football. You spend Sunday afternoon watching the pro games, and Sunday night at a coaches' meeting. I never see you."

"But, honey," Ted would counter, "you knew I was going to be a coach."

"If I had known living with a coach was going to mean living alone, I might not have married you!"

And so it went.

Janeal became more and more unhappy. And when friends at work invited her to stop by a bar for a drink on the way home she welcomed the chance. It wasn't that she liked to drink; she didn't. But at least she wouldn't be alone. Soon one drink led to another, and for several months these occasional stop-offs became a regular habit. But then one night, a friend had to help Janeal to her car because she had gotten so drunk she had forgotten where she left it, and the next day she had no memories of how she got home.

This episode scared her, and like a hard slap in the face, it woke her up to how destructive her lifestyle had become. She gave herself an emotional shake and pulled herself together. She cut back on drinking and treated Ted with more kindness. Whatever this was that had taken hold of her after the miscarriage needed to be thrown off *now*.

In a little while she was pregnant again. The nine months were a rerun of the all-day sickness she had felt with the miscarriage. She even got sick on the way from the labor to the delivery room, but their son was born healthy and sweet and beautiful. Janeal had given her husband a son! Never in her life had she felt so fulfilled. "The pregnancy was awful," she told Ted, "but if I knew I'd get this same result, I'd do it all again. It was worth every bit of the suffering!"

After Richie turned two, the time seemed right to try for a second child. But Janeal's body did everything but cooperate. It had something to do with her menstrual cycles, but neither she nor her doctor seemed to know what. Her cycles would be sixty-five days apart, then eighty-three days, then seventy-two days, then fifty-nine. And the irregularities couldn't have been induced by her birth-control method; she wasn't using any. Even the unpredictable cycles would have been tolerable if she didn't also feel so dreadful. Periodic nausea, no energy, tenderness in her breasts, times of sharp cramping. She gained thirty pounds and lost all her sparkle. More than once she called her doctor's office, wondering if she could possibly be pregnant. But they would always advise her to wait and see, and by the time a pregnancy test was scheduled, her period would have started.

The next years passed in a physical and emotional blur so draining that there was no time or energy to think of Ted. When Janeal did, she didn't like what she saw. Hungry for a companionship she wasn't supplying, Ted had slipped into the drinking-with-friends trap she had tried a few years before. It started as an occasional night of bowling with the guys. But those evenings out began stretching to midnight and beyond, and then into breakfasts.

The realization of what was happening rocked Janeal. Ted was a coach and didn't even believe in drinking. Their life together must have really slipped for him to do what he was doing. She would just have to change things—and she would! She tried the "best-wife-I-can-be" routine; Ted didn't respond. So she switched to nagging. Nothing changed. Then yelling, screaming, threatening. But their relationship only got worse. And the cold reality of their failure came to a head the day that six-year-old Richie asked them, "If you guys get a divorce, who would I live with?" They had never talked divorce, but even their little child could see what was happening and where it had to lead.

Janeal began to panic. And it was little consolation when her doctor finally decided that her physical trials the last few years stemmed from the fact that she *had* been pregnant after all, probably several times. "Apparently the Pill wasn't the only factor in your earlier miscarriages," he told her. "You probably conceive easily enough, but your eggs aren't strong enough to carry the pregnancy to term." And he offered a medication she could try that would, he said, "strengthen the eggs." But the responsibility for another life was the last thing Janeal wanted as she felt her life sliding into a downward spiral. And she opted instead for having her tubes tied.

The day of her tubal ligation, as she lay on the preparation table, she asked the nurse to call Ted. But as the nurse turned toward the door, Janeal stopped her. "Never mind. He wouldn't care . . ." And the nurse came back to her side. Two more times she would ask for Ted, and both times change her mind before he could be called. What she longed for was that he would burst through the door and stop the proceedings. "I love you, and want us to have more children—and a life together," he would tell her. But she knew it was nothing but a fantasy. Their lives by that time were moving hopelessly apart.

Why she called her sister-in-law that afternoon in May she wasn't sure. They lived a hundred miles apart, and the call was long distance, but Janeal somehow knew she had to phone. After too many minutes of chit-chat, Janeal got ready to hang up. "Wait a minute," Lois caught her. "Do you want to tell me why you really called?" "Why? I was just in the mood for a visit," Janeal lied. Her sister-in-law could read through her defense and attacked it head-on. "Come on, Janeal. You called me *long distance* at 1:00 in the afternoon just to chat? What's the real problem?" Janeal was silent. "It's Ted, isn't it?" Lois asked. Janeal sighed deeply. "Yes." But as Lois probed for specifics, Janeal held back, not knowing where to begin. It had all become so complicated and confused and overwhelming.

Lois and Scottie had been through their own set of struggles, so Lois understood better than Janeal knew. And as she gently began to verbalize Janeal's tangled feelings, Janeal wept, first from relief that someone, at last, actually understood her pain. Then she cried from the realization of such failure. And Lois went on to explain the answer she and Scottie had found. Turning her life over to Jesus Christ could mean a new start. "I've tried all I know to keep my life under my own control," Janeal wept, "and look at the mess it's become." And in a broken prayer, she offered her life to God. "I don't know if you can heal our marriage, or put our lives back together," she admitted to God, "but I do know I simply can't handle my life anymore. Please do with it what you want." She felt tired, but not with the life-draining exhaustion of the years before. This was more like a relieved collapse into the arms of a Loved One after the struggle is over.

The first indication that her prayer had tapped her into the resources of God happened less than a week later. At a Memorial Day family gathering, Lois's husband handed Ted a magazine article on Christian marriage and suggested he read it. So Ted lay down right then on the floor and did. When he finished, he looked up at Scottie with a different expression. "Thanks, Scottie!" he shook his head, "I needed that." And with that, he pushed himself up off the floor, walked over to Janeal, and took her in his arms. For months Janeal had ached for him to initiate a tenderness like this toward her, and now here it was. But his embrace was to be just the first outward sign that something changed in Ted as he read that article. He promised that he would never drink again, and he kept the promise, even through a long summer with his old friends. And the new expressions of love and caring for Janeal and Richie continued.

In the days ahead Janeal and Ted spent long hours talking about what was ahead, and where God would fit into it all. Little by little they agreed *together* that Christ would be the director of their home. They began to rebuild their marriage, this time from a solid foundation. The dark clouds of depression lifted, and their lives together began to reflect God's peace and love.

As the hurts started to heal, and their love grew, Janeal began to feel stirrings inside her of desires for a baby. With her ugly history of sickness and loss, she was amazed at the realization. But there was the problem of the sterilization. "Perhaps it can be reversed," she thought. And she scheduled an appointment with the only surgeon in the city who was attempting the procedure. There was only a seventy percent chance of reconnecting the tubes, he told her. Then just a sixty percent chance of becoming pregnant and less than fifty-fifty odds of carrying the baby to a healthy delivery. Janeal and Ted talked it over. Could they take the disappointment if it didn't work?

After several months of agonizing over the decision, they decided they could, and Janeal called the surgeon's office to schedule the operation. But the doctor, the receptionist informed her, had died! Janeal was sure she'd heard wrong. The only doctor in the city doing the surgery had *died*? As she hung up the phone, it was as if God spoke to her, "Janeal, you've asked Me to guide your life. I do not need your help. Stop trying to manipulate circumstances so things will work out your way, and just trust Me." Janeal's mind flashed back, back to the time when *she* had decided to go on the Pill, and *she* had decided it was time to have a child, and *she* had decided to have her tubes tied. Now *she* was deciding to have another baby. All of this deciding had led to nowhere but heartbreak. She would let God decide and accept whatever He chose. In the meantime, there were others who needed her, and not just Ted and Richie.

There was the friend of a friend whose marriage was shattering, just as Janeal's had been. Janeal got to see the sharing of her own journey point the woman to a new life in Christ. And then there were Dave and Rita. Dave's busy medical practice had pulled him away from Rita and their four children. And Janeal and Ted were able to love and encourage Dave and Rita back toward Christ and His life for them.

Dave's phone call came as a surprise that April afternoon. "What can I do for you, Dave?" Janeal said as she cradled the phone against her shoulder and dried her hands on a towel. Dave laughed. "I think it's what I can do for you, Janeal. Do you still want children?"

Janeal's heart skipped a beat. She had casually mentioned to him once that if he ever came across a patient who needed to give up her baby, to keep them in mind. He did call once last year to say they were second in line for a baby, but the first-in-line couple adopted the child, and they were left disappointed. Could he be calling with another possibility?

No, surely not. Janeal shook herself a bit to re-enter reality. During Dave and Rita's marital problems, she had kept their kids a lot, and she had no regrets. Besides the satisfaction of knowing she was giving Dave and Rita much-needed time to get reacquainted, she and Ted absolutely loved those kids. The days with those four little boys gave Ted and Janeal their first taste of how much they could love children who weren't even theirs. Yes, it would be great to see the kids again.

"Children. Sure, Dave. How many?" she responded.

Dave knew then she hadn't understood what he meant. "Just one, Janeal. One healthy, beautiful, newborn baby boy. A patient of mine wants to give him up for adoption. She has two children already, but her marriage is breaking up, so she feels she just can't support another. She had planned to place him through an agency, but now she's changed her mind. Now that she's had him, she can't bear the thought that he won't be placed immediately, that he could be shifted from one home to another until he's adopted. She just wants to know he's settled. So, of course, I thought of you."

He had a baby for them? The thought was staggering. The dream she had longed for, now possibly here? But equally staggering was the flood of "what about's" his offer precipitated. What about Richie? He had enjoyed eleven years as an only child. How would he react to their family expanding overnight? And what about her work? The typesetting business in her home had mushroomed from an occasional assignment to an all-day-nearly-everyday demand. She had enough work waiting in the office now to take up two weeks. Where would it all fit? She mumbled something to Dave and asked if she could call him back. Her hands shook as she dialed Ted's number at school.

"Ted, we need to make a decision." She didn't know how to begin, how to tell him. "Can't make a decision without me, huh?" Ted teased her, but her voice didn't pick up on his banter. "You don't understand, Ted. It's kind of a *lifetime* decision. Dave called, and he has a baby boy we could adopt. Honey, we need to let him know in forty-five minutes if we want the baby or not."

There were seconds of silence on the other end of the line. "Richie's here with me. We'll be right home," Ted finally said.

"But what if Dave calls back before you get here?" Janeal asked. "What am I going to tell him?"

This time there was no pause. "Tell him that *of course* we want the baby!" and the phone clicked. Janeal sank into a chair, relieved and dazed. And if she had had questions about Ted's sincerity, *or* Richie's enthusiasm, they all vanished when the two burst through the front door. "We've named him!" Richie yelled and hugged her. "He's going to be Peter Jeremiah, and we're going to call him P.J.!"

Their dinner was no dinner. Janeal couldn't cook . . . couldn't eat . . . so Ted and Richie fended for themselves. A friend was scheduled to come that evening for Bible study with Janeal. "Should I tell her not to come?" Janeal wondered. But then she'd have to explain why, and what if, somehow, the adoption didn't go through. Better to keep quiet until the baby was actually theirs. But concealing her churning hopes and fears wasn't easy. She could barely focus in her thoughts as they opened their Bibles.

But as she scanned the page before her, a particular verse virtually leaped out to Janeal. "In love He predestined us to *adoption* . . . through Jesus Christ to Himself, according to the kind intention of His will, to the praise of the glory of His grace."[1] Reassurance from God! And later that evening, Dave and Rita stopped by with their own reassurance. Rita had been allowed in the newborn nursery, and had actually gotten to hold their baby. "Oh, Janeal," she gushed. "He's got fat, pudgy cheeks, blue eyes, and he's already got your name written all over him!" The baby would be released Wednesday, Dave told them, so they would have Tuesday to make final arrangements with their attorney and pick up the baby things they'd need.

However, Tuesday morning at 8:15 a.m., Dave called. "Janeal, things are moving faster than we expected. I'm making rounds at the hospital, and the baby's mother wants to go home today. But the baby has to be released when she is. You'd better stay by the phone because you're going to be getting this child today, and it may be anytime." Today? But they didn't even have diapers. And Janeal couldn't call anyone to help out, because they still didn't want to leak the news until their son was safely home. So she rummaged through the few momentos she'd kept from Richie's infant days. One ratty baby blanket, one outfit, one bootie. It would have to do.

At 11:00, their attorney called. "Be at the hospital at one o'clock with an infant car seat, a change of clothes for the baby, and two witnesses," she instructed. Janeal could barely think of her own name, let alone accomplish a list of chores. But she managed a jubilant call to Ted, and the two of them raced off to

---

[1] Eph. 1:5, 6a, New American Standard Bible.

grab a car seat at a department store, and head for the hospital parking lot. Just as they started out the door, the phone rang. It was a printer she knew well, asking for help on a rush job. "Oh, Dick, I'm sorry. Any day but today. I'm on my way to the hospital to get a baby." The printer heard the phone click, but looked at the receiver a moment before hanging it up and turning to his assistant. "I think Janeal just said she was going to the hospital to get a baby! I didn't even know she was pregnant!"

When Dave placed that little boy into Janeal's waiting arms, both she and Ted simply melted with love for him. "Who could ever have dreamed a bonding could be so deep, so complete?" Janeal wondered.

For the next two weeks, people poured into the house to see Peter Jeremiah, bringing love and gifts and best wishes. Of course Janeal and Ted had nothing prepared for the baby, but that weekend they moved Ted's office out of the skylight bedroom and downstairs. Wallpaper, paint, furniture—a nursery was born. And friends filled it with all the necessities until the gifts and baby things overflowed into the living room. Their church hosted a shower, and sixty-eight ladies came, with another eighty contributing toward larger gifts. People brought dinners and came to help clean house and just share in the joy of this miracle. Friends from around the country called to wish them well. And Richie relished the role of the undeniably proud big brother.

"Peter Jeremiah is an incredible gift to us," Janeal reflected later. "And he's such a reminder to not be afraid to trust God. When I was making all the decisions, our lives only went wrong. But when God has freedom to handle things *His* way, He makes beautiful things happen."

Have you thought of adopting?

You've heard, I'm sure, that fewer babies are available for adoption now than have been in the past. More unwed mothers keep their babies, and a million and a half mothers a year choose to abort their children. Both factors add up to a lessened availability of adoptable children. But as Janeal and Ted's story proves, it is still possible to adopt. The question is, should you?

Though adoptive parents will tell you that there are many facets to consider in the should-we-adopt question, one stands out boldly: *What do you expect an adopted child to do for you?* Your answer will tell much about whether or not adoption should be a consideration.

An infertile woman I know was rightly outraged at the suggestion she apply to adoption agencies as an aid to becoming pregnant. Her well-meaning advisor reminded her that sometimes women who have tried for years to conceive choose to adopt a child, and then bingo! They're surprised by a pregnancy. "If you adopted," the person went on, "the pressure you feel would be off. Maybe then you'd conceive like you so badly want to."

"And what if I did conceive?" my friend asked me. "Would the adopted child then have served his purpose? Do I then send him back?"

Adopting a child is, indeed, a poor method, for trying to work out your frustrations and helplessness over pregnancy loss. For Janeal and Ted, there was a time when adoption would have been very wrong. When their own marriage was shaky and their personal lives in upheaval, they had little to give to anyone. They needed to set their own house in order before sharing it with another. Because they did, Peter Jeremiah could be loved for himself. He was not saddled with a hidden set of expectations no person could fulfill.

Other considerations unique to adoption need to be explored as you consider a course of action. Those who've done it say the best resource for finding out these issues are adoptive parents themselves. Talk to those you know. And read. One excellent Christian adoption agency highly recommends Jacqueline Plumez's book *Successful Adoption: A Guide to Finding a Child and Raising a Family* (Crown, 1982).

Starting the search.

As the Neilsens looked for a child, they tapped an obvious source: the Yellow Pages. Calls to the adoption agencies listed led them to interviews with their state department of social services, and then to private adoption agencies like Catholic Charities and Lutheran Social Services. They found that adoption through the state agency would cost them nothing, but the majority of the children were older, handicapped, or had been in foster care for extended periods.

Adoption through many of the private agencies would be expensive (usually around $5,000—not to "buy a baby," but to pay hospitalization for the mother and other related expenses), and if they held out for a Caucasian infant, the waiting periods ranged from three to six years. Some agencies had special regulations, according to their governing boards. Catholic Charities, for example, gave priority to Catholic families. Some church-affiliated agencies required a particular doctrinal statement from the parents. Agencies varied in their expectations.[2]

The Neilsens eventually considered foreign adoption, and after a wait of only six months, are now the proud parents of handsome, lively, Korean-born Matthew.

After you have made the rounds of agencies, a private adoption like Peter Jeremiah's, arranged without agency involvement, might seem too good to be true. Certainly, in these privately arranged adoptions, some parents have gotten the children for whom they have longed without that five-year wait.

But there is another side to the story. The Christian Action Council, headquartered in Washington, D.C., encourages unwed mothers seeking to place their child for adoption to go through a reputable agency, if at all possible. Barbara Hammond, coordinator of their Crisis Pregnancy Centers, explains why. "In some states, private adoptions can take place with no home studies of the adoptive parents being done. And even though these couples are absolutely convinced they'd be wonderful parents, and their attorney may agree, there may be factors in their home life that only an experienced observer can catch. In agency adoptions, home studies are done before, and then for six months after the adoptions." Also, in private adoptions, no counselling is usually provided for the mother giving up her child. In an agency place-

---

[2]If you seek more information about adoption agencies (religious and secular), a listing is available from the National Committee for Adoption, Suite 326, 1346 Connecticut Avenue, N.W., Washington, D.C. 20036.

ment, necessary counselling is more often provided for."[3]

For the mother, too, there can arise the sad situation of delivering a child with birth defects, and then having that child rejected by the couple who had been committed to adopt the baby. If the mother had gone through an agency, provisions would have been made for the child, even if birth defects were present.

Private adoptions are not always flawless for the couples involved either. One family reported having lost nearly $12,000 over the last few years trying to get a child. Four different times they paid for the medical expenses of a mother, expecting to adopt her child, only to have the mother change her mind after the child's delivery. Some state laws give the natural mother up to a year to change her mind about the adoption, even after the child has been placed.

But private adoption is still, to many couples, an attractive alternative to agency adoption. It sometimes affords them a baby they might not have otherwise had.

The ultimate source.

The fear hit Janeal five days after Peter Jeremiah's arrival. A newspaper article set it off, a story about a natural mother surfacing at her baby's five-month birthday to reclaim her child. And Janeal wept brokenly to her attorney. "It will happen to us, I know it. Anyone who knows how wonderful this baby is will insist on having him. And I couldn't part with him. I couldn't."

But the resolution of these fears did not rest in legal information, reassuring though that was. It came back to the basic question: where did the child come from? He came from God, Janeal knew. Whatever *God* does, endures. Janeal was reminded

---

[3]The Christian Action Council (422 C Street, N.E., Washington, D.C. 20002) has pregnancy crisis clinics in all fifty states. Though not an adoption agency, they can refer you to reputable agencies in your state that might be adoptive resources. One such agency they recommend is Bethany Christian Services (901 Eastern Avenue, N.E., Grand Rapids, Michigan 49505). Bethany is established, reputable, and with offices in twenty states, offers a variety of services, including the opportunity for international adoption. Another recommended agency is the Evangelical Child and Family Agency (1830 North Main, Wheaton, Illinois 60187).

to give Peter back to God, not hold him clutched to herself.

Our sovereign God can overrule in "impossible" situations, regulations and shortages, not withstanding. One couple in California agrees. They were 500th on the waiting list to adopt a child. Five hundredth! But, as they waited, in a neighboring county, a pregnant girl filled out the forms to release her child for adoption. For religious preference she penned "born-again Christians." Neither she nor the couple knew of a national law which insists that a mother's religious preference be honored, no matter what it is. And the county in which she lived had no "born-again Christians" listed among their perspective adoptive parents. So officials made a call to a neighboring county which passed over five hundred applicants to connect with the couple who shared this mother's religious leanings. After all, the law was the law! And a surprised and grateful couple rejoiced at the child God had given them.

God is the giver of children. If you're considering adoption, look to Him for direction. Ted and Janeal would tell you it is the only way that makes sense.

CHAPTER THIRTEEN

Fulfillment Is Not a Just a Child Away

Fifteen years ago Myrl Glockner was stumbling in a fog of sorrow and confusion after repeated miscarriages and stillbirths. And when her pregnancy attempts ended, there was no glorious story of a miracle adoption to follow. The Glockners are childless. But neither Bob nor Myrl would use the word "less" to describe any part of their lives. They instead come up with terms like "full" and "abundant" and "adventurous." In one of those little life summaries we all do from time to time, Myrl looked back over the years and said, "I often feel like God's spoiled child!"

How did she come to feel this way? And what perspective does she have for us, this lady who endured eight pregnancy losses and never saw her dream of having children completed?

Losses remembered.

Waking up in a hotel in Hong Kong. For a woman raised on a Wisconsin dairy farm, it should have been exhilarating. But the excitement of this exotic setting was lost in the disappointment Myrl felt after miscarrying there in their hotel room, the night before.

Perhaps losing the pregnancy shouldn't have come as a surprise. For one thing, Myrl had been living under the pressure of an incredible schedule. This Hong Kong stopover was just one in a series through the Philippines, and Taiwan, then Tokyo and

Okinawa as she and Bob worked their way back to the States after five months in Australia. Bob worked for the Billy Graham Evangelistic Association, and during the stint in Australia, was teaching classes and doing set-up work in preparation for an upcoming Leighton Ford Crusade there. It was a lifestyle they enjoyed, she freely admitted, and one they were to continue for the next four years. "Religious gypsies, that's what we were," Myrl would laugh later. "Living out of our suitcases while we traveled from one ministry assignment to another. Hotel rooms became as familiar for us as most people's living rooms are to them. We really loved what we were doing, yet at times we longed to settle down in a home of our own."

The time in Australia, however, had been one of their more demanding assignments. Between speaking engagements of her own, Myrl served as Bob's on-the-road secretary. And she had kept a hectic pace from city to Australian city, even after she knew she was pregnant. It became more difficult as morning sickness plagued her 24 hours a day. So maybe the stress on her body caused the loss.

For another thing, there was her age. Women of thirty-two years experiencing a first pregnancy *ought* to expect a bit of difficulty, she reminded herself. That's simply one of the drawbacks of not marrying until thirty. But it was one of the very few drawbacks. She had spent her twenties in a whirlwind of exciting and fulfilling service, her time divided between the Billy Graham Evangelistic Association and the Navigators, another Christian organization. And it was during those years that she had met her husband, also a Christian worker. She smiled as she looked over at him, still asleep.

She knew Bob enjoyed children. They'd spent the previous summer in Switzerland with a family of seven, and Bob became a Pied Piper for the entire clan, making up games, planning events. The kids had liked her, she knew, but with Bob, it had been a love affair! This man was born to father. They'd simply have to try again.

Two years and four more trips later, Myrl was pregnant once more. But this time they decided on more caution. Bob would go alone to Canada to work on the Leighton Ford Crusade, and she would stay with her sister in Minneapolis. Three months . . . four months . . . five. Myrl finally boasted one of the wonderfully round pregnant-woman figures she had only envied before. And she felt the wonder of their baby moving inside her. Bob and Myrl eagerly discussed possible names as the creation of this new life forged an even deeper bond of love and joy between them.

But only days later, Myrl would watch her tiny son die. The loss began with a harmless looking show of blood. By the time of her examination the next day, however, Myrl's cervix was dialated to nine centimeters, just one centimeter away from full dilation! An "incompetent cervix," the doctor called it, one too weak to withstand the pressure of the growing baby's weight. But they would try to save the child. Myrl was admitted to the hospital and placed in bed with her feet elevated in the hopes that the baby would recede back into the uterus. If it happened, the doctor would suture around the cervix and sew it closed for the remaining months of the pregnancy. At that time, this particular procedure was fairly new, so her doctor gave no guarantees. At least it was a chance. "Please! *Any* chance!" Myrl pleaded silently.

But the procedure didn't work. Within a few days, the protruding membranes had become infected, and it was clear that the baby would not make it. He lived for just five minutes after the delivery, and for months Myrl could close her eyes and see his tiny body, there in her doctor's hand, shivering and struggling to breathe. Everything in her cried out to hold him, to breathe for him that he might live. They named him Robert, after his father, but privately they called him "Robby." And they wept together over his death.

It was two years before Myrl became pregnant again. And in the years after there were two pregnancies that went to six months, and four three- and four-month miscarriages. Physicians diagnosed her problems as "varied"—once cervical incompetence, another time an infection in the wall of her uterus. And a hysterectomy later on showed signs of adenomyosis, a condition in which the walls of the uterus thicken and become porous like a tumor, resulting in inevitable abortion at some point in the pregnancy.

Perhaps they could adopt children, friends suggested. Bob

and Myrl applied to an adoption agency, but their lifestyle was no asset. Instead of a picket-fenced stability, their record showed hotel after hotel as their home. So when the agency rejected their application, the Glockners were disappointed, but not surprised. Two different times opportunities for private adoptions arose, but each time the baby would have arrived in a matter of weeks, and each time the Glockners had neither the living situation nor the financial means to take a child on such short notice.

After a decade of attempts, Bob and Myrl accepted the fact together that their dream of having their own children was not going to become a reality.

What were the struggles?

Even though she was deeply committed to God, Myrl was plagued by the same "whys" of any woman who has lost a child. As she recalls:

"Once, just in passing, my doctor wondered if there might be some psychological factor causing all these losses. And when he said that, it sowed a seed of doubt that stayed with me through the rest of the pregnancies. I began digging around in my attitudes and emotions, trying to uncover some hidden subconscious reluctance that was bringing on these losses. Could there be some sin in my life, some bitterness toward God or some other person that was keeping me from childbearing? Or perhaps I wasn't being allowed to have children because I simply wasn't fit to be a mother. Anything seemed possible.

"And at a crusade in Canada, I sat next to a woman whose husband had been miraculously healed of a critical illness in answer to prayer. When she learned of my pregnancy problems, she insisted that I could have delivered each of those babies safely if I had only had enough faith. Any self-condemnation I had felt before suddenly quadrupled. Had lack of faith on my part made my dear little ones die?

"One of the biggest struggles with these was-I-at-fault questions came after the death of one of our little boys six months into the pregnancy. It was a particularly sad loss because he lived for some two hours, and I had some particularly emotional moments with him just after the delivery as he lay on my stomach. He was so big, and he looked so normal. That parting came hard.

"Although my doctor indicated that total bedrest would make no difference in the outcome of that pregnancy, some well-meaning acquaintances made it clear that if I had stayed on my back the entire time instead of going ahead with the Bible classes I'd been teaching, I probably could have carried him safely to birth. They were sure of it.

"Oh, how I agonized over that one! Our first Bible Study Fellowship class was just beginning in Minneapolis, and we were ecstatic at the 350 women who were growing and changing through the class. Should I have reneged on my commitment to the women who needed me, when I believed God had led me to teach? Would it *really* have made a difference in the outcome of the pregnancy?

"And I ached at the realization that because I couldn't bear children, Bob would never have the joy of being a father. When Robby died, Bob's first words to me in the recovery room were assurances of his love and of his complete contentment with me, even without children. But a moment later, he turned away toward the window, and I realized he was crying. But he kept his sorrow at simply sorrow. It never turned to blame or any hint of disappointment in me. And I longed to return his loving acceptance with the children we both desired."

And there are still times when the hurts persist. "Christmas always has a tinge of sadness about it, bringing back memories of the two Christmases spent in labor rooms preceding a loss. Though our families are so aggressive and gracious to include us, we're always fitting into someone else's holiday. It's a reminder that these might have been days when we would have enjoyed Christmas with our own children. Then there are those times when I'm meeting someone new, and the inevitable 'How many children do your have?' question surfaces. And I see their faces fall when I tell them we have none. But these times pass. I see them as just little 'life pricks' that help keep me humble."

And now, a decade after her last pregnancy, Myrl has come away, not bitter, but better. She feels a sense of loss as she remembers the miscarriages, but the pain is gone, and in its place is honest joy. "It's not that I'm glad for the suffering itself," she says. "But God has taken that suffering and through it produced so much good that I am glad for having gone through those losses. This deeper pain has somehow opened in me a capacity for deeper joy."

Finding peace.

What does Myrl tell women about finding the peace she has found? She shares four suggestions.

1. *Grieve, but don't waste your grief.* "A few days after Robby's death, the magnitude of the loss finally hit full force. I had driven Bob to the airport to catch his flight for Canada, and as I pulled into the driveway of my sister's house where we were staying, I could tell I was falling apart. As I often do when my emotions are shaky, I headed for the piano to play some hymns, but I only managed a few bars of the song before I began sobbing. I needed to grieve, and I let myself grieve. Fortunately, I was alone.

"But at the same time, I was determined that this grief not disintegrate into a whining self-pity that would shut me off to God and to people. And it could have happened.

"When the doctor first told me I might lose the baby, everything in me wanted to shout, 'No! I *wanted* this baby, and I will have this baby—whether God decides to help me or not!'

"But in the three days that followed, as I lay immobile on the slant board waiting for an outcome I knew I couldn't control, I had time to think and to remember Jesus in the Garden of Gethsemane, facing an agonizing death on the cross. He could ask His Father to spare Him the pain, but He said instead, 'Not *My* will, but Yours be done.'[1] He relinquished the outcome to His Father, knowing full well the possible cost of choice. But He submitted, because He believed the Father's way was best. 'For the joy set before Him,' the writer of Hebrews says, Christ endured the cross.[2]

---

[1] Luke 22:42.
[2] Heb. 12:2.

"I needed to release my child to God with a commitment that whatever the outcome of his life, I would trust God to do right and that good would come to us all through it. Once I said yes to God, that He could do with my child's life what He thought best, incredible peace flooded through me.

"And over time, I began to see Him take the hurt and use it as a vehicle to develop a new sensitivity and a new tenderness in me, both toward God and toward others who were hurting. Instead of hardening me, the sorrow made me softer and better equipped for the life I was being called to lead."

Feel your grief, Myrl advises, but don't let it harden into bitterness and cynicism. If you do, you'll have squandered what could have been an invaluable resource for good in your life.

2. *Share the fullness of your hurt with God.* "Run to the arms of your loving, caring Heavenly Father, and pour out your pain to Him," she encourages. "Someone once said, 'Tell the Lord all about it,' and from that reminder I've often found healing. Friends can sympathize, but they can never provide the depth of comfort and healing available through Jesus Christ. During the years of losses, I recall so often opening my hurts to God and then seeing Him soothe and heal my aching heart. God longs to comfort us, but we need to go to Him."

3. *Let God supply the answers you need.* Myrl is convinced that God has particular answers for each of the hurts we encounter, and that our responsibility is to go to Him with each of them as they come up, asking Him to help us view the hurt from His vantage point.

"I remember so well the man's comment," she recalled. "I listened because he was a minister of missions, and I listened because he was a friend. But he said, 'Myrl, I feel your ministry to others is going to be limited because you don't have children.'

"His prediction cut like a knife. I could recall as a girl of eighteen, looking at a little motto so carefully hung on the wall of my parents' home. It read, 'Only one life will soon be passed; only what's done for Christ will last.' And I longed that that motto would characterize my life. One great consolation in these pregnancy losses was that perhaps they were equipping me to better serve Him, to better reach out to others. Now this respected man of God was tearing from me a hope I had clung to. My ministry would be *less* because of these losses, not more.

"For a time, I simply accepted his assessment. After all, how does a woman without children minister to those who have them? How could these women ever feel that I understood their problems when I've not been part of a life experience of so much significance to them?

"But Jesus Christ had a different perspective on this issue. And when I turned to Him for *His* answer, He reminded me of Henrietta Mears, a Bible teacher who influenced dozens of prominent Christian leaders—all men, and yet she was a woman. And there as A. Wetherall Johnson, the founder and director of Bible Study Fellowship. Her godly life has affected hundreds of thousands of mothers. Yet she was not even married!

" 'Myrl,' the Lord instructed me, 'your ministry does not begin with your qualifications or your life circumstances. It comes from who you are inside and how deeply you abide in Me. The fruit in others' lives depends only on how much you let Me live through you.' "

Ask God for His perspective on your pain, she says, and wait for His answer. Refuse to settle for anything less.

4. *Don't live to be happy. Live for God, and happiness will follow.* Myrl notes, "Though my days are full of joy, I've learned that fulfillment and happiness are not worthy life goals. And they are certainly not my life goals. Fulfillment comes as a by-product of a life of obedience to Jesus Christ, so that's where I've focused. I've held tightly to God's promise that 'if you are willing and obedient, you will eat the best from the land.'[3]

"And I've drawn instruction from David's perspective, 'In Thy presence is fullness of joy.'[4] It comes from living in His presence. And there is no joy in life greater than knowing the reality of God, and in seeing Him work through me in the lives of others.

"Many of the women who've been helped through Bible Study Fellowship in Minneapolis over the years have told me that they

---

[3]Isa. 1:19.
[4]Ps. 16:11, King James Version.

know why God hasn't given me children. They remind me that I could not have had the ministry I've had if there'd been little ones to be responsible for.

"But an even more satisfying answer to me is simply that the God of the universe intended that for me, a life without children would best fulfill His plans. Does that make a difference? It certainly does! This One I serve does all things *well* after the counsel of His own will, and I'm living the life He designed for me. Any other life would be less, not more."

Living in Joy.

Like Myrl, many of us have found Jesus Christ to be sufficient to meet the pain of pregnancy loss.

Jill told me, "It's been three years since our miscarriage, and I still cry sometimes when I talk about it. But you know, so much spiritual growth came from that painful experience that I almost don't regret having had to suffer." She went on to explain, "Before my miscarriage, I knew about God. I knew what the Scriptures taught about His faithfulness and His help in time of need. But after losing the baby, I experienced the reality of His healing for myself.

"Watching Him reach into my grief and transform it into peace gave me eyewitness assurance that He is worthy of my trust—and my life."

There is a future for you, a future filled with hope. Your life ahead may hold natural children, as it did for me. Or adoptive children, as it did for Lynette. Or spiritual influence, as it has for Myrl. But if you put your past and your future into Jesus Christ's care, you can discover, as others have, His capacity to create from your pain beauty and joy and completeness. I know it.

God bless you.

REFERENCES

"Are You Positive about Your Rh Blood Factor?" Booklet published by the National Foundation of the March of Dimes, White Plains, New York.

Berg, Barbara. *Nothing to Cry About.* New York: Seaview Press, 1981.

Church, Martha Jo; Helene Chazin; and Faith Murray Ewald. *When a Baby Dies.* Oak Brook, Ill.: The Compassionate Friends, Inc., 1981.

Crow, James F. "Immunogenetics." *Genetics Notes,* 8th ed. Minneapolis: Burgess, 1983.

Friedman, Rochelle, and Bonnie Gradstein. *Surviving Pregnancy Loss.* Boston: Little, Brown and Company, 1982.

Good Housekeeping's Family Health and Medical Guide. New York: Hearst Books, 1979.

Green, T.H. *Gynecology, Essentials of Clinical Practice,* 3rd ed. Boston: Little, Brown and Company, 1977.

Jackson, Edgar N. *When Someone Dies.* Philadelphia: Fortress Press, 1971.

Klaus, Marshall, and John H. Kennell. *Parent-Infant Bonding,* 2nd ed. St. Louis: C.V. Mosby Company, 1982.

Lakes, Ross A. "Five Good Reasons to Show Caution in Giving," *Christianity Today.* April 20, 1984.

McCown, Darlene E. "Children and Death." *Light and Life* magazine. April 1984.

Miles, Margaret Shandor. *The Grief of a Parent When a Child Dies.* Oak Brook, Ill.: The Compassionate Friends, Inc., 1978.

Peppers, Larry G., and Ronald J. Knapp. *Motherhood and Mourning, Perinatal Death.* New York: Praeger Publishers, 1980.

Pizer, Hank, and Christine Palinski. *Coping with a Miscarriage.* New York: New American Library, 1981.

Pritchard, J., and J. MacDonald. *Williams Obstetrics,* 15th ed. New York: Appleton-Century-Crofts, 1976.

Rosenblum, J. *How to Explain Death to a Child.* Booklet.

Schiff, Harriett. *The Bereaved Parent.* New York: Crown Publishers, 1977.

Tengbom, Mildred. *Help for Bereaved Parents.* St. Louis: Concordia Publishing House, 1981.

Wells, Robert G. "The Hidden Costs of the New Genetics." *Moody Monthly.* June 1984.

White, Karol. *What to Do When You Think You Can't Have a Baby.* Garden City, N.Y.: Doubleday and Company, 1981.